T0354930

# THE LIGHTHOUSE KEEPER

TREVOR RENWICK

Order this book online at www.trafford.com
or email orders@trafford.com

Most Trafford titles are also available at major online book retailers.

Print information available on the last page.

ISBN: 978-1-4120-8958-6 (sc)
ISBN: 978-1-4122-0728-7 (e)

Because of the dynamic nature of the Internet, any web addresses or
links contained in this book may have changed since publication and
may no longer be valid. The views expressed in this work are solely those
of the author and do not necessarily reflect the views of the publisher,
and the publisher hereby disclaims any responsibility for them.

Any people depicted in stock imagery provided by Getty Images are models,
and such images are being used for illustrative purposes only.
Certain stock imagery © Getty Images.

*Trafford rev. 07/05/2024*

 www.trafford.com

**North America & international**
toll-free: 844-688-6899 (USA & Canada)
fax: 812 355 4082

# DEDICATION

I dedicate this little book to my wife, my friend,
my lover and my soul mate.

Joanne

Forever, and a day.

Cover Photo – Me!

# INTRODUCTION

It has been a lot of fun and I am still only 59. I am not a great explorer or a famous figure or even a mildly famous figure. I am just a simple soul born in England in 1946 who has had the good fortune, and maybe a bit of luck, and maybe even a touch of stupidity, to have been blessed with a life that has led me all over the world and to have met the most wonderful people, done some really interesting things and also to have experienced the disappointment of knowing some really stupid people. I should not forget to mention the overwhelming power of testosterone, which has driven me forward across whole continents.

I have done nothing world shattering to date but I still have a few years to go.

This is not a work of fiction and neither is it intended to rattle the literary world.

I have always thought that everyone has a story to tell so this is my attempt to tell my tale and who knows, maybe I can add a chapter or two before we can write;

## The End

Why did I call this book 'The Lighthouse Keeper'?

This is an interesting and amusing little story that almost sums up how a young lad, growing up in Middle Class England has no real direction unless he conforms to the norm. The norm being a safe, homely, debt laden existence in England's green and pleasant land. Hey – Don't get me wrong here. There is nothing wrong with that and it happens to suit most people. Little holidays in Mallorca. Going back to the office with a ten day tan. Maybe even one of those bonking holidays in Ibiza – lead me on Jimmy!

No – not only my parents, but even the mighty UK

government realised that this lad was a bit strange. Not in a funny way. Quite serious really. Or I was then. I learnt much later not to take life too seriously.

Anyway – where was I ? Ah yes – Lost. Lost is what I was. No other way of looking at it.

All of 18 years old. Not clever enough to follow in my fathers footsteps in the medical world. Too sickly – if you call suffering from hay fever being sickly – to do my Biggles impressions in the Fleet Air Arm. Not even BOAC would have me. So bang goes my adolescent dreams of a white silk scarf and a Tally Ho life.

I needed guidance so I went to that 'all powerful', 'all knowing', Government Department – The Careers Advisory Bureau. I had seen their brochure in the school library and being an independent young soul, off I went to seek their guidance. I remember that a rather plump man in an ill fitting tweed jacket with slightly frayed sleeves interviewed me and listened to my tales of academic mediocrity. Not too many 'O' Levels and barely scratching past with a couple of very mediocre 'A's, there I was.

I could do all kinds of other things though and at that time I considered that these were far more important. Being able to ride a horse or being a good shot or a good canoeist was far more important than a few official papers saying 'O' Level Geography – Pass.

Maybe my tales of prowess or my enthusiasm for my non academic life gave my interviewer the insight he needed. I think that our interview only lasted about 30 minutes but he had me summed up by then. No question about it. There was one career that would suit me down to the ground.

LIGHTHOUSE KEEPER

Maybe he was right.

# PREP SCHOOL

I don't really remember much about my early youth. I was born in October of 1946 shortly after my father came back from the war. Not much of a story there except that when I was growing up and imagining myself following in my fathers footsteps and being a doctor I used to read up on all kinds of things medical and one of the charts my father had was a pregnancy conception dates chart. I secretly got the chart from his office and started studying it. After all, this had something to do with sex. I was not quite sure what, but even the thought of studying such a chart set my little adolescent heart pounding.

Conception! Ahha – I know what that means. Giggle giggle.

Then I looked up my birth date and worked back to – yes – the date of conception. There it was in black and white – date of conception – 1st January.

That's it! I was not planned, I probably was not even remembered – Yep – New Years Eve. Just the result of a drunken frolic. Hey Ho.

My mother later confirmed my worst suspicions – I was her delightful surprise. Don't tell my sisters though.

My father was extraordinarily proud when I was born. Apparently, he was running around telling everyone that he had a son – yes, a son. Must have been something to do with his Cumberland hill farming upbringing. Survival of the species and all that.

So I don't remember being conceived and neither do my parents – ha ha.

I do remember that we lived in 'Doctors Road'. That was 'The Crescent' in Linthorpe, Middlesbrough. Everyone on that road was a doctor. Strange. Maybe they were trying to set up their own little empire. Knowing what I know now and how incredibly sensitive English people are to appearances and status maybe that is not too far from the truth. Mind you the houses were not grand. Big, yes, but definitely not grand. The grand stuff came afterwards for the ones that made it. My parents were really not like that and maybe a bit of that rubbed off on me and my sisters. If so – thanks. No great ambitions for social status to be chased. No screaming desires for wealth. A happy life, not really bothered about what other people thought.

I think I must have been a bit of an embarrassment sometimes though. I was always a bit wild and I really had no comprehension about what was 'the done thing' or 'not the done thing'. Our next door neighbour from those days still remembers my attempts at the Boy Scout 'Bob-a-Job'.

I was an expert drain cleaner early in life and that was my expertise at the tender age of 6 or 7. So that was the service I offered. Nobody else would do it. My opening lines during 'Bob a Job' week – 'Excuse me – may I clean your drains?'

Playing in the back alley in Welly boots in the rain, sweeping torrents of water and great big waves down the central cobbling – Wow – now that was fun.

Yes – not the thing to be seen doing in our neighbourhood but my parents never discouraged me so I went my own little way making waves and cleaning drains.

I must have gone to 'Prep' school at about the age of five. I don't keep dates but I think that was the norm. It was one of those lovely, oldie-worldy' Prep schools where your mastery of Latin was the key to a successful life.

'No stopping that lad – he can quote from 'The Aenead'. Ahaa – and yes, his father was in The Forces of course. Old England's not finished yet.

Red House School in Norton – apparently it is still going strong and is still quite good.

What was lovely about that school was that it was a day school and mixed. None of that 'keep them separate for their own sakes' stupidity. What did we know then? Girls were girls and they had their own sports because we boys were tougher and stronger. But – but there was a sneaking interest which intensified as the years marched on. Interest, but not obsessive. So we drilled a little peep hole in the changing room wall so that we could take it in turns to see the girls getting ready for gym or whatever. So what? Healthy interest I say.

The girls were just as bad. Standing at the end of the long jump pit on sports day before we lads realised what a jock strap was. I thought they were there to cheer me on to break the school record.

Actually, it was a nice school and a nice time. One of my best friends in those days was the beautiful Andrea. What a magnificent woman. All of 8 years old.

I suppose that the friendships that form at these early years are almost instinctive. You feel a bond between friends that happens naturally. Maybe you are of like mind or maybe you just like to run and play. Television was only just becoming available and we did not have a set at home for many years so our fun was cycling over to see friends. Running, chasing, playing games, cowboys and Indians. Bang Bang – you're dead or I'm not playing.

Yes – I had fun – and I learned Latin.

Now cycling was not something I did for healthy exercise, it was my only form of independent transport. I must have cycled thousands of miles, literally. My dream was to own a racing bicycle and this was my stated wish on my 8th birthday. I don't think my parents really understood. Maybe they didn't know the difference between a *racing bike* with *drop handlebars* and a normal bike. I was so sure that I was getting a racing bike that I was quite a brat when I was given a normal straight handlebar bike with a three speed 'Sturney Archer' hub gear system. Do you remember them? I haven't seen one for years. It had a tiny little chain that went into the centre of the gear hub and moved some cogs back and forth. But, being a brat, my dream was to be bent down over *drop handlebars* and be cycling at break neck speed on a *racing bike*. How could I cycle at break neck speed with straight handlebars? You see, they really did not understand.

But boy-oh-boy how that bike would go. I was a daring little soul at 8 years old and learnt to make the most of this 'touring' bike. I cycled everywhere. I cycled back and forth to school every day come rain, sleet and snow. There were about three or four of us who used to do that run every day and we had an ongoing competition to see who could go the fastest. We could even overtake cars. Our little skinny legs would be pumping away and we would fly.

Jonathan Livingstone, schoolboy.

Those cycling days went on for many years. In fact I think I was still cycling pretty much everywhere I went until I was about 19. I even went to our little local snob group dinner dances on my bicycle. I would have my little metal bicycle clips to hold my trouser bottoms off the chain and a Macintosh to keep the worst of the weather off my junior dinner suit and off I would go to dance the Cha Cha or the Foxtrot with Andrea.

Aaah – what joy!

Amazingly, accidents never seemed to happen although we had a few close shaves. One famous run to school we had been tearing up the road to Norton and we arrived well ahead of time so we were fooling around on our bikes when one bright spark bet that we could not ride our bikes with our hands crossed over so that the left hand was on the right handle and the right hand was on the left handle, if you see what I mean.

If anyone ever tries to bet you on this one, just let it go.

They are right – it cannot be done. Over I went, right in front of a large lorry that was coming up behind. Screeching of brakes, angry words from an angry driver but not a scratch on me. Dust down with lots of laughter and not a care in the world.

How is it that my parents never worried? Maybe that was the start of my wanderings. They showed absolutely no concern about where I was or where I had been. It was not lack of love or a careless attitude. It was as if they had consciously decided that this was the best way for kids to grow up and learn to stand on their own two feet. Maybe they trusted me or maybe that was the way to grow up.

Don't misunderstand me here. I was not allowed to run totally wild and I did have certain restrictions. Bedtime was very strict and I was under strict instructions to be home by a certain time. I also had my homework to do and both my parents made sure that I set aside enough time to do it. It is just that every opportunity that I had I was out on my bike and away.

Time passed in a happy carefree way until those dreaded exams – 'The Eleven Plus' started to loom over the horizon. Maybe some kids can cope with this academic pressure at such an early age but I certainly couldn't. I don't think that I really understood the need for academic accomplishments. I still considered being able to ride a horse or catch fish with my bare hands far more important in Trevor Renwick's Grand Scheme of Things. But obviously the rest of the world did not agree, so I did my best.

I know that I scraped by in most subjects with the exception of Latin of course– at which I excelled, but my results were not a huge cause for celebration at home.

The 'Common Entrance' exams were just as bad but I think I had a slightly better idea of what was expected of me by then.

My father was a clever man and I don't think he really understood why his son struggled to achieve these academic targets. He always encouraged me but I think he was secretly a bit disappointed that I was not 'top of my class'. I think that his ideas of success were still deeply entrenched in his hill farming background in Cumberland and the usual ambitions of 'What I want to be when I grow up' were still limited to those pillars of society, – doctors, lawyers and bank managers.

There is a very amusing little anecdote that one of my father's partners told me recently that gives some insight into my father's character and his way of looking at life.

My father had two partners in his practice. All three of them were very good doctors, by all accounts, but each of them had very different personalities.

One of his partners, John Whewell was a very bright, academic man who took great pride in his attention to detail and making sure that all the 'T's were crossed and 'I's dotted.

His other partner, David Strachan, was a little bit more relaxed but none the less a very good doctor who took great pride in his work.

My father, on the other hand, the good old Doctor Robert Hilton Ralph Renwick, was very much in touch with the world around him. He was well loved by his patients and had a wonderful sense of humour. He always appeared to be quite serious, but under that skin of respectability, pillar of society, and all that kind of Methodist upbringing stuff, I suspect that there was a simple country lad more 'at home' in the countryside than in the hustle and bustle of towns and cities.

The story goes that one day someone asked them what time it was.

John Whewell looked at his watch and declared it to be 12.37.

David Strachan also glanced at his watch and said that it was about half past twelve.

My father got up, went outside, looked up at the sun and stated that it was early afternoon.

Another wonderful character trait of my father was his attitude to the environment, nature and conservation. While driving, he would suddenly brake or swerve to avoid hitting any birds that might be peacefully pecking at grit in the road. I leave this one to your imagination. Newspaper headlines:

"Two sparrows – Only survivors of a multiple car pile-up on A1"

He would have fitted right in with some of those animal rights groups.

So, there I was with my not very impressive 'Eleven Plus' and 'Common Entrance' exam results and I think my father had to pull a few strings to get me into a good public school. His first choice for me had been Epsom but my results put me a bit down in the list. I was not accepted there but I was accepted at Durham School which was the second choice.

In the mean time life was marching on at my Prep School and the testosterone was just starting to course through my veins. The girls at school were starting to blossom and little hints of breasts and shape were starting to emerge. Now this was interesting and I found my self drawn to this wonderful new experience of adolescent desire. I think that at this age it was more an inquisitive desire than a full blown testosterone rush.

I had already taken my first date to the cinema at the tender age of 9. I was a well brought up lad so I politely knocked on the door of her parents house and asked if I could take Rosemary to the 'pictures'. I escorted her to the bus stop where we caught the dark blue double decker bus to take us to the cinema. I think I tried to kiss her in the back row of the stalls but I really hadn't got a clue what I was doing but there was a sense of pride and accomplishment that I had taken the lovely Rosemary to the cinema.

Friendships grew and I sometimes regret that I let those friendships lapse as the years passed.

I never kept in contact with my friends from those days and I often wonder what happened to them. Are they happy? Have they had a good life?

I suppose it would be unrealistic to suppose that we would have much in common after all the experiences we would all have had by now.

Sad that those wonderful days of carefree, youthful, joy and laughter and friendship are a distant memory. It is a closed chapter in all our lives I suppose.

Nice memories though, so hold on to them and let's move on.

Before I close this little section on 'setting the scene' I think that I should just say a word or two about my mother, Betty Renwick. She came from the south of England which was always looked at with suspicion by those hardy folks from the north. 'Toffee nosed snobs down there you know'. 'All got bloody plums in their mouths'.

She was born Betty Evelyn Barker and grew up in Bedford.

Her wedding photograph shows her to be a tall, dark haired beauty and my father looks incredibly proud.

She seems to have shrunk considerably over the years.

They met at the early part of the WW2. My father had been posted to West Africa with the Royal Army Medical Corps and he was on leave when a friend of his arranged this blind date for him. He was quite a short man so he probably needed some help.

The story goes that the date was a success but he never followed up on it and away he went again for another tour of duty in The Gambia and Sierra Leone. Obviously, he did not see much action in those days and I think that he spent most of his time running a clinic for the locals and the nearest he got to any action was shooting snakes.

On with the story – apparently during this tour of duty he started to write to my mother and arranged to meet her again when he got his next leave. This he did and apparently he wasted very little time before he asked her 'What about it then?'

How's that for romance? I can just see my father charming his way into a young girl's heart. Ha ha.

I have a sneaky suspicion that my mother was not quite as innocent as she would like us to believe. Her worldly mind quickly questioned the 'What about it then?' as perhaps a subtle suggestion to jump into bed.

But no – what my father meant to say is 'Will you marry me?'

When they eventually got these translations sorted out she did weigh up the pro's and con's and she agreed.

What is interesting is that after a very short honeymoon my father was once again posted off to active service in North Africa and later Italy and this time it was a bit more serious than shooting snakes in The Gambia and Sierra Leone. As the air raids around the south of England intensified my mother moved up to my father's home village of Garrigill in what is now Cumbria. Garrigill is a cold, wet, windy, tiny little village up in the Pennines. Not a lot goes on up there and 80% of the tiny population of two hundred or so carry the name 'Renwick'. I suspect that there was very little in the way of transport either into Garrigill or out of it over the centuries.

What is amazing to me is that my elder sister Linda was born up there and three years later my father came back for the first time since they got married, to meet his three year old daughter. That needs to be thought about for a while as it gives a bit of insight into the characters of my parents. I wonder how a young couple would cope with that nowadays. Never knowing if your partner would be coming back and precious little in the way of communication. Just the odd letter and three years away. That shows some commitment and loyalty. Love might just sum it up.

So – I think that this is enough of the background to my tale. It is time to move on as there is a lot to tell and the exciting bits are still way down the road.

# Public School

My time at Durham school is not one that fills me with particularly joyful memories.

It was a boarding school and we were only allowed home for one day every three weeks.

It was one of those old long established public schools with an impressive history. Founded by King Henry VIII, etc., and closely associated with the Cathedral. 'Founders & Benefactors' and all that.

I think that when I went to Durham it was the first time I had ever really met any 'nasty' people (I was to encounter a lot more of these as the years passed). Typically these were young men with ambitions. Very strange thing – ambition.

I can understand how someone wants to achieve something, or become really good at something, but sadly most ambitions seem to be too focused on getting ahead of the pack and trampling anyone and everything in the way. It is an ambition for 'power' that really scares me. Power – what for? To use for what? I see politicians taking acting lessons to better convince (or fool) the public. People and 'leaders' avoiding telling the truth or simply twisting it in their favour. For what? Power? When I see people at the end of their lives, bed ridden or so destroyed by Parkinson's disease or by Alzheimer's I think, what a stupid waste of time it must be to have these kind of selfish ambitions to have power or to 'get ahead' which even by definition is pretty sad.

I feel a bit guilty that I did not enjoy this time at Durham or maybe even make the most of it as it was agood school and I know that my parents had to make some financial sacrifices to send me there. Boarding schools are not cheap and it must have cost a small fortune over the six years that I was there.

Hey Ho – let's dwell on the lighter side for a while.

I still hadn't really got into the academic side of things at school. My mediocrity from Prep school followed me to Durham, except of course for Latin. At the end of my first year exams at Durham I got 96% in Latin. If Latin had been a sport I would have got the school record and probably still be holding on to it. Maybe Latin would be my saviour.

Latin for the Olympics – Gold Medal and fame for Trev!

It was not that I was dumb; it was simply a case of my attitude to learning academic subjects. As long as I could scrape by then I would devote my energies to other interests.

It was as if these targets of 'O' levels and 'A' levels were merely a hurdle that had to be crossed. You did not have to take a massive jump to get over and neither did you need to 'train' for hours on end. The hurdle was set at a height that I could get over – but only just. Anyway there was still plenty of time before I had to tackle these exams so why not put all this 'swotting' aside for the time being. Whoops – Bad mistake Trev lad!

In the mean time my interests lay with sports and activities outside the classroom. I had always been a good shot and my father had brought me up to respect the rules and dangers of shooting. So I joined the school 'small bore' shooting club. This had a little 25 yard range at the back of the School Cadets Armoury and we used to practice there every week. We used some rather old Mossberg .22 rifles and also the old Lee Enfield 303's converted down to .22. I was rather good at this and became school captain of shooting.

In fact I still have a small trophy at home when Durham School won the northern counties small bore competition. Not bad.

There was a very funny incident at this rifle range one day.

Our shooting coach had come to the range with a very fancy target rifle with all the knobs, whistles and bells that these things have. If you have seen one of these you will know what I mean. They are quite big and heavy considering that they are only .22 calibre but they have all these little nooks and crannies and holes in the stock to put your fingers through. Real Star Wars stuff.

They also have what is called a 'hair trigger' which is adjustable so that you only have to put the slightest pressure on the trigger – and bang – off she goes.

Our coach, who spoke in one of those rather high pitched, very posh, straight out of Sandhurst, accents was demonstrating how tightly the actual bullet fitted into the breach of this fancy rifle. He was extracting the bullet from the breach and was showing us the rifling marks on the bullet. To do this he had the muzzle of the rifle resting on his foot so that he would not scratch his precious gun on the floor.

Yes, you guessed it – as he went to close the Martini action of the breach, his finger must have touched the trigger. ----- Bang!

Oh dear me – ruined his shoe.

It was quite amusing to see this very posh twit hopping around on one leg shouting at the top of his voice

'My God – I've shot myself – I've shot myself'!

I rushed off to get Matron who was a short rotund stocky lass but really there was not much she could do. She wrapped a small bandage neatly around the perforated foot and told him to drive himself to the hospital. Shame about the shoes though. There was a neat little hole all the way through and a black powder burn on the uppers. I don't suppose he ever used those again.

My other 'love' at Durham was canoeing and I was rather

good at it. I went on one of those Central Council of Physical Recreations courses up in the Lake District one summer. It was skilful and physical and although you do rely to a certain extent on other people it is an individual's sport. There was a group of about six of us from school who did this course and we managed to get canoeing integrated into part of the School Cadet Force. So instead of having to polish our army boots and spend every Thursday afternoon marching up and down to the orders of a sergeant major from the Durham Light Infantry, off we went to the river to polish up our 'Special Boat Service' skills.

We built our own glass fibre canoes, as well as one Eskimo Kayak. This was a very thin, long canoe which was ideal for doing all the 'Eskimo rolls' and other tricks.

One day we were all down at the river which was in flood and we were using our canoes to shoot down a channel at the edge of the weir. This 'sluice' had a slight turn in it half way down and the little slalom canoes could get down quite easily. We had the long Eskimo Kayak with us and I foolishly suggested that it would be fun to go down in that but I thought that the turn in the sluice was a bit too sharp for this long kayak. I forget who it was, but one of the team piped up that it was easy – he had already done it lots of times. Okay – this lad doesn't need any more encouragement, so off I went.

I must have looked a complete idiot stuck fast halfway down this sluice with the kayak firmly wedged, front and rear, with mountains of water pouring over me. The only way out was to abandon ship which I did to the roars of laughter from the other lads.

We had a good little team in this club and we spent every 'Field Day' shooting rapids or paddling out to sea. We learned how to rescue each other far out at sea and how to do summersaults in the waves as we surfed in. Not quite loop the loop but close.

Damn but we were good.

We used to put on shows all around the North East of England and became quite an attraction at swimming events and regattas. One of the little tricks to try to upset the crowds was to capsize and then very gently get out of the canoe while upside down and then surface with your head inside the canoe so that you could breath the air inside. The commentators were in on the act and would start to sound worried after a minute or so and would allow a touch of panic to come into their commentary after two or three minutes.

After about four or five minutes when the crowd was convinced that you had drowned, you would very gently summersault back into the canoe while upside down, secure the spray deck and then roll the canoe upright.

'How did he hold his breath for so long?' – Wow. Applause. Fame.

Our canoeing coach was very good and had been involved in coaching the British Olympic team so he knew a thing or two. He had a famous saying that 'Panic is fear of the unknown – therefore we are going to get to know the unknown'. His voice matched the saying. He had a deep gravely voice with a broad North of England accent. No frills or airs and graces on this lad.

It was a valuable lesson and did actually save my life later in a canoeing incident on the River Tees.

It was another of our Cadet Force Field Days so we had taken off to the river while the other poor sods were climbing mountains and shooting blanks at each other.

At the end of a series of rapids, which we had been playing around in, there was quite a nice waterfall with a drop of about four to five feet which is quite exciting when you go over it in a canoe. We were having a lot of fun going over this and then getting out and carrying the canoes back up and then going down over it again. All good fun and quite spectacular and

21

there was quite a crowd of spectators gathering on the banks of the river to watch this.

Just after the waterfall the river split into two streams and we had been going down the right side as this seemed to have more water in it. After a couple of shots over the waterfall I decided to try the left hand one just for fun. Unfortunately, (you knew that was coming didn't you?) there was a large rock in the middle of this part of the river and I totally misjudged the swirling current and came up hard against it with the river pouring over me and the canoe. I was well and truly wedged there and could not move the canoe at all due to the force of the water. Time to get out of this, so I pulled the spray deck back and stepped out. There must have been a large deep section of the river right there for my feet did not touch bottom and down I went with the canoe on top of me. The canoe was now pinning me down and the force of the water and the weight of the canoe, full of water above me, was too much for me to move it. I was under water at this point and I could see the coloured hull of the canoe above me so I wrapped my arms around the part of the canoe that I could see and pulled like mad to get my face above water and yell for help.

What was really dodgy about this was that nobody was watching this part of the river as all the fun and excitement was up at the waterfall which was a good fifty yards or so upstream.

I don't know how many times I had to haul my head out of the swirling water and yell but eventually I felt two strong hands under my arms pulling to get my head back above water. It took another couple of helpers to jump into the river and get the canoe off me.

All this took quite a while but eventually I came out of it safe and sound. I know that if I had panicked in that situation I would not be here now – so coach – if you are out there anywhere – thanks. It was a good lesson.

There is a funny thing about this little incident. At the time I did not really think much of it. I kept my head, I did what had to be done and I came out of it so it was not a big deal.

I think that it was some time later that I realised how close that had come to a disaster.

Rowing – yes -I was good at that as well and managed to get onto the First Eight. Our coach for rowing was our Housemaster – Mr. DeW. – I can't remember his first name.

He had Brylcreamed swept back hair and also had one of those annoying high pitched 'plum in the mouth' type of voices. Whenever he got agitated he would brush his hair back with a sweep of his hand and he did that quite a bit. He was a very good rowing coach and we did train very hard. A typical day for the First Eight would be a six mile row followed by circuit training followed by four runs up the chapel steps. That last bit was a killer as the chapel sat high on a hill and there were something like 350 steps to the top. Do that a few times at full throttle and you know about it. And we used to do that every day and twice on Sundays!

So we were incredibly fit and strong. Rowing uses just about every muscle in your body and when you 'explode' off the front stops you are putting in the maximum effort into that stroke. It is a team sport in a way but not the same as rugby or football. Each rower lives in his own little world of effort and pain and all he has to do is keep his timing right and his balance. I think it suited me, as did canoeing.

The school had been given a brand new 'Eight' by some benevolent rich father or maybe an 'Old Boy'. These boats are rather expensive and they are made with the finest materials. It must have cost a fortune. DeW. decided that we should try this new 'Eight' out on a 'Long Course' which is about a four mile row upriver, going against the current. All went well until we were quite a way up river beyond the normal regatta course. We were screaming round this corner going at full welly as we 'gave her ten'. Full throttle – that is, for you non-rowers out there.

What DeW. had forgotten was that it had been a very wet winter and there had been several floods early in the year. There was a sickening crunching and thumping sound as the brand new 'Eight' grounded at full speed onto a new gravel bank just below the water level., ripping the bottom out of the boat and leaving us all looking very stupid sitting there with water swirling around our ankles in this sunken, wrecked, masterpiece.

DeW. was screaming from the banks brushing his hands back through his Brylcreamed hair.

'My God – The river's changed course, the river's changed course'

(He always repeated himself in case you didn't get his message the first time round)

Yep – it sure has Einstein.

Those days at boarding school were rather strange as you were locked up at this school for seven months of the year and then you were on holiday for the other five months or so.

It was a very black and white situation for me.

Time at home on holidays passed very nicely. I had my bike, the open roads and I was as fit as a fiddle. I think I must have taxed my parents' patience though. I was at that awkward age of rebellion. Thinking that I was smart and clever. What a pain in the arse!

I think my parents must have been quite used to bringing up children by now as I had an elder sister who also 'did her own thing', but she was much brighter than I was so probably didn't get into so much trouble.

All our lives we had a 'cottage' as a holiday home. In the early days this had been close to Garrigill. You remember that one, the 'Renwick' village with the transport problems. Well we had a lovely but very ugly, square cottage up there on a hillside. It was called 'Waterfall Cottage' and somehow my father had managed to take a long term rental on this for the princely sum of 30 pounds per year. It had no electricity and no running water and we loved it. The River Tyne flowed along the valley at the bottom of the hill and off to the North there was a tributary that flowed over several large waterfalls and into some dark peat coloured pools. The water was absolutely freezing of course but I made a raft out of pine tree trunks and I would happily play around in these freezing waters. Launching assaults on imaginary forces or exploring imaginary jungles.

We used to play with the kids from the local farm and they taught me how to tickle trout and run at breakneck speed along the river, jumping from stone to stone.

Another favourite of ours was hay making time. The cut grass was piled into 'pikes' to dry out and when it was dry and ready,(which could take an awfully long time in Garrigill) it was Hay Making Time.

The old grey Ferguson tractor would go out with a flat decked 'bogey' to collect these 'pikes'. The bogey would be backed towards the pike and then the pike had to be pulled on board using a chain and a hand cranked winch. We would then all pile on board and bounce our way back to the farm, hanging on for grim death, where the pike was pitch forked into the barn. Great fun.

My mother eventually got tired of the incessant rain and cold weather in that high, wind swept, part of the country and persuaded my father to rent an old farm house on the other side of Cross Fell in the Eden valley, close to Ullswater. This was really a step up as it had running water and after a while we had electricity put in. Luxury I tell ye!

It is funny to think that in those days it was only we poorer folks that had cottages.

All the well off people went to stay in hotels for their holidays.

I think some of my parent's friends felt sorry for the poor Renwicks.

'Going off to stay at their cottage, can't afford a proper holiday you know'.

'What do they do with themselves all day, way out there in the country?'

Now it is the other way round.

The cottage in the Eden Valley was in a village called Blencarn and it was owned by our 'Auntie' Christine. She was not a blood relative but did claim some dim and distant relation through some 25th cousin half removed – I think you might know the type.

She was a strange old duck was Auntie Christine. She had grown up – guess where?– in the village of Garrigill when my father was still a lad there. I never did get to the bottom of that story but there is a story, I am sure. Nothing was ever said but I think she was still secretly in love with my father. (I add the *'still'* there on the assumption that there was a little tale from little old Garrigill that never got told)

Auntie Christine was a divorcee but in reality she was born a spinster. She did try one short marriage but it was doomed to failure.

'After all, he didn't even clean the guns properly'

'What kind of a despicable bounder this poor chap must have been'.

Christine was not shy in coming forward and she had been

known to bare her breast to my poor father on the pretext of some minor medical ailment. Probably in the hope that the mere sight of this ageing bare bosom would fill my father with uncontrollable desire and off they would ride into the sunset. Ha ha, what a wonderful picture.

Our little old farm house or 'cottage' in Blencarn became quite a den of iniquity as we got older. My friends and I would have some wild old times up there. I suppose my parents guessed but they still let us get on with our lives. One morning there must have been about twelve of us staying there and all the girls were down in the kitchen preparing breakfast. Good old Auntie Christine must have seen some activity from her house across the fields and not taking any chances, she loaded her double barrelled 12 bore shotgun and marched across to the cottage. The first thing anyone knew was this rather short, stocky, power house of a woman burst into the kitchen and levelled her gun at the crowd in the kitchen and demanded to know 'Is Trevor here?'

The poor girls nearly had a fit. They gave me some very strange looks for the rest of the day believing that this 20th century Boadicia was a relative of mine.

So there I was having fun, growing up slowly and spending my years in this rather strange world of prison at school, alternating with freedom during any holidays.

When I was on one of my school holidays at about the age of fifteen I met my first real flame. Wendy. Wendy and I were about the same age and she was extremely beautiful and had a body to die for. All the lads wanted Wendy as a girl friend. She was the catch to go for and she was MINE – ALL MINE I TELL YOU!

I used to cycle (of course) over to her house at Eaglescliffe, which is a fair old hike, and we used to snog for hours on end.

I use the word 'snog' on purpose. How on earth did we all do that? We barely came up for air and this snogging went on, and on, and on. I think that there was a secret hope that if you kept snogging long enough it would turn into something else. Jee whiz – what stamina. Every night I would cycle over to Wendy's house and the snogging would start and not stop until I had to set off back to Linthorpe. Hours were spent in these youthful amorous embraces. But it wasn't the hugging or embraces that amaze me – It is the non stop kissing – I think that snogging is a better way of describing this as it bears little resemblance to kissing.

I was incredibly proud of Wendy and I know that all the lads were very envious. She was stunningly beautiful with long dark hair and the most beautiful body you could imagine.

My imagination at the age of 15 or so was firmly fixed on breasts. Anything else was in a dark unknown and unseen area so I just concentrated on what I could see and hopefully eventually feel – and that was – breasts. And Wendy had wonderful breasts – wow – I kept up the snogging for hours on end, hardly coming up for air, but I had a purpose. Sooner or later I was going to feel those breasts.

We kept this youthful innocent relationship going for quite a few months. It might even have been a year or more. Love letters were exchanged during my imprisonment at Durham and a couple of times I actually escaped and hitch hiked down to see Wendy for the day. I was besotted and I was willing to take risks.

Actually I never got caught and my status in the school notched up a few points with my daring escapes to see the beautiful Wendy. I was not shy of showing her photograph around either. Eat your hearts out lads.

Well, as you can no doubt imagine, these long drawn out snogging sessions gradually progressed into some mild petting, then into some heavy petting until the day arrived when we both lost our virginities.

What a palaver. What a struggle. What a disappointment to both of us. What a shame.

Virginities should be lost under instruction or at least one partner should know what they are doing.

It was a pity that we were not old enough or confident enough to laugh it off and have another go

I wonder if that is the same for most people.

Our relationship seemed to tail off from that point on. I think that we were both a bit secretly ashamed and feeling guilty as we were still quite young. So we gradually drifted apart and went our merry ways. No more love letters and a short break for me to find another snogging partner.

I must have been attracted to Eaglescliffe because my next girlfriend lived there as well so I continued to rack up the miles on my bike and continued to try to polish up my snogging skills.

But at least this time I had the name right – Jo – This time it was a Josephine but I would refine that over the years to come to find the right Joanne.

I won't bother you with more drawn out details of life at Durham School although there are lots of tales that I am missing out. Some of them funny and some not so funny but I think you must have the gist of it by now and it is time to move on.

I eventually managed to rack up 11 ''O'' levels by a series of takes and retakes. Distinctions in Latin of course. But I made a bit of a mess with my 'A' levels and made a complete shambles of the Biology exam which was the 'A' level subject I was best at. In hindsight I wonder about the actual value of those academic qualifications. Most of the more valuable lessons I was to learn later in life had very little to do with my ability to dissect the endocrine system of a rat. It doesn't even make a good topic of conversation for dinner parties does it? Maybe it was a way of training the mind or 'rounding off' the person or maybe it's just a way of keeping you occupied as you are going through that awkward adolescent stage in life.

Do you know – I have never ever been asked to produce those 'O' level or 'A' level certificates. Strange after many years of studying nobody really seems to care.

# OTHER LESSONS LEARNT

Another valuable lesson that I learnt during my years at Durham was that subtle relationship between 'Work' and 'Money'. In hindsight it was probably one of the most valuable lessons I learnt in my adolescent years.

My father was not mean, but he did believe that you should earn your way and he introduced me to the horrors of having a Social Security Number and something called 'Tax'.

When I was about 16, I had come home from school for the summer holidays and I told my parents that I wanted to buy a motor bike. My father did not bat an eyelid and did not even bother to correct the glaring error in the use of 'I' where it should have read that I wanted *him* to buy me a motor bike. Subtle difference there Trev lad.

He expressed an interest and asked me how much I thought this would cost. I had done my home work and I knew the make, model and the second hand prices. No doubt about it – a Triumph Tiger was the bike that he should go out and buy for me.

He looked out of the window and seemed to ponder for a while. He asked me again how much I thought that this would cost and I happily walked into the trap –

'Yes, I think I can get a good second hand one for about 30 pounds.'

'Well', he said, 'if you go over to Moore and Cartright's building site a few streets away there is a job waiting for you' and he was sure that after a few weeks work as a labourer on that site I should be able to afford to buy this motor bike.

I don't know how he knew this was coming or whether he just decided that it was time for me to try my hand at working and actually experiencing the thrill of getting a little brown envelope at the end of each week with a few bank notes and coins in it.

Earned by my own blood and sweat. Wonderful.

My first attempt to earn and save some money had started and quite frankly it was a very good lesson and never again would I be reliant on my parents' generosity for my 'Play Money' anyway. All my holidays from then on involved some kind on menial job to put some coins in my pocket but needless to say I did not get that motor bike that year and neither for several years after that.

Working on this building site was quite good fun actually. I was still a bit of a toffee nose but not a twit and definitely not a snob. The building site workers took the micky quite a bit, but in a nice way. But they did give me some shitty jobs to do. –Literally. I won't upset you with the details but they all got a good laugh out of some of the jobs they made me do. Hey, I didn't mind – after all I had good training in this. Remember the Bob-a-Job drain cleaning six year old!

After this first baptism into the real world I never had any problems getting work during the school holidays and I was already working out which job would pay best and also an interesting little quirk crept into my choices – which job would be the most exciting?

As this tale progresses you might catch a hint of this more and more as the tale unfolds.

So I did the building site labourer, demolition worker (Remember what Stockton High Street looked like before 1965) and all kinds of other manual labour during my 'hols'. None of that office work for me. Outside and roughing it. Macho man (boy).

Another good lesson and fun – so thanks Dad.

# EXTREMES

Now before I finish this little section I just want to tell you a couple of wonderful tales that might give you some insight into where this story is going. I know most people don't believe me when I recount these stories, but they are true, and I enjoy telling them.

After my father had kicked me out of the house that famous summer holiday to work on the building site I managed to get work of some kind on most of my holidays from school. This young lad is not dumb and I had already done some research on the jobs that paid best and had the least hours. Guess what came top of my list – 'Dustbin Man'.

Yep – that's right. Marvellous money. All of eleven pounds a week!

Hey, don't scoff, that was good money in those days.

The other great thing about this job was that you only had a fixed route to cover each day so the faster you went the earlier you finished. So, if you lived around the Acklam area in about 1962 and you were puzzled why the dustbin rubbish was all over the pavements and the roads it was just me trying to learn how to run while spinning those old metal dustbins on their rims. Quite skilful actually and it does take a bit of practice.

My parents did not know that I was doing this job and it came as a bit of a shock to them when they learnt. They actually found out from a friend of the family.

I was now an expert at running with these bins and I was collecting the rubbish from an area quite near to home. Unfortunately, one of the bins had a jagged rim and this caught on the front of my trousers as I span it towards the truck. It ripped the whole front of my trousers away leaving my milky white thighs exposed to the elements and the public. As a proud dustbin man you cannot go around half dressed. Not the done thing at all.

So, it was rescue time and I knocked on the front door of 'Auntie' Margaret who lived on that road. It took a bit of explaining as you can probably imagine as I stood there with the dustbin lorry behind me and my brilliant white 'Y' fronts shining in the morning sunlight but she gave me a couple of safety pins to patch up my trousers and cover my modesty and back I went to running and rolling those bins.

If we went fast enough we could be finished before midday which was great. It was actually good fun to be roaring through the countryside and villages hanging onto the back of a dustbin truck. It was also quite an eye opener to work with the dustbin men though. Some would even eat as they worked, if you see what I mean. I won't elaborate.

The other extreme was my 'relationship' with the Royal family.

Yes, that's right ER II and family.

I thought that might get your attention.

I think it must have been about the same year that I did my dustbin man impressions.

Somewhere around 1962 or 1963 I got a call from a shooting buddy of mine, John Dickson to ask if I could help him out. John was at St Andrews University studying medicine. Each year the lovely Queen Mum would ask the students at St. Andrews if they would work for her as grouse beaters for eight weeks up on her estates up by Balmoral. Every year ten lads and ten lasses from St. Andrews would go up there to plod over the wet, cold, windswept moors, walking about 16 miles a day, making funny whirring and clicking noises and waving white flags to scare the grouse into flight and to 'guide' them or 'drive' them over the Lords and Hierarchy armed with their Purdeys and Holland & Hollands.

John was short of a beater that year and as I knew a thing or two about grouse shooting and 'beating' he asked me if I could come up to Balmoral to make up the numbers. Anyway, I came to the rescue and volunteered my services.

I did this for four years running, eight weeks at a time for most of the years, and thoroughly enjoyed it.

The Queen Mum had kitted out some stables at Abergeldie Castle on the south side of the river Dee between Balmoral and Ballater and that is where we stayed. The Queen Mum was very proud of what she had done at Abergeldie Castle and she told us that she had chosen the shower fittings, curtains and other furniture items herself. Nice touch I thought. What a lovely lady.

The Queen Mum actually stayed at her own estate at Birkhall which was nearer to Ballater.

Every four weeks the Queen and Royal family would have what is called the 'Gillies' Ball' at Balmoral Castle. This was specially for the household staff and we, Abergeldie Beaters, were always invited as well. There was a very strict dress code at these events as it was imperative that the Royals did not mistake us, peasants, for one of their own. So all the Royal Family and their guests would be dressed up in their finery but we peasants, we commoners, had to wear nothing more formal than lounge suits. Over the years it became a bit of a habit that John and I would always dance the Dashing White Sergeant with HRH Princess Anne and I would dance the Gay Gordon's with her. Protocol dictates that you cannot ask a member of the Royal Family for a dance, they must send their Lady In Waiting across to ask you to dance with them. I don't know how HRH managed it, but she always made sure that John or I were available whenever those two dances came up.

Obviously, there is a story or two to tell here. One of the funny ones was when four of our Abergeldie girls got lost in Balmoral Castle just before one of these Gillies' Balls. It would have created a major terrorist scare nowadays but back then things were a bit more relaxed.

On with the tale. We peasants had to arrive and be in the ballroom before the Royals made their appearance, which they did down a pair of staircases at the end of the ballroom.

When we arrived these four girls went to powder their noses (or whatever) and apparently they took a couple of wrong turnings and ended up in the private quarters in the castle. Somehow they found their way to this 'Royal Entrance' to the ballroom and as they opened the door the massed peasants assembled below fell into respectful silence.

I can't remember but I have an awful feeling that the band even broke into 'God save the Queen' as they started down the official staircase.

Whoooops!

Another 'Whooops' happened at Abergeldie Castle one weekend when we were not out on the moors 'beating' the grouse. I had a little Berretta .22 rifle which I used to bag a few rabbits from time to time to help out on a food supply. As I was heading out of the stables, John told me to pass by the main part of the castle (which was deserted) as he had seen some people in the grounds and they must be trespassers. As I approached the castle I could see two ladies, bent down and peering in through the windows.

If I had taken more time, the fawn trench coats and scarves should have warned me.

But not me – trigger happy Trev.

'Excuse me ladies', I shouted, 'This is private property'.

You know what's coming, don't you?

36

As they turned around to see who was shouting at them my heart sank.

What have you done Trevor lad?

Yes – it was the Queen Mum and ER II!

"Sorry – apologies – it's your castle – look as long as you like – would you like a rabbit for the pot?"

Bow. Scrape – walk backwards Renwick.

Of course they were very decent about it and I did not end up in The Tower or on the chopping block

Then the next year we almost did the same thing again. We were driving through the grounds of Balmoral in a little old Mini to go to the private golf course. There ahead of us walking down the road with her back to us was a lady in another fawn trench coat and scarf. I did not see the Corgie, neither did John, and I had completely forgotten my previous lesson on the warning signals given out by fawn trench coats and scarves.

Before I could stop him, John put has hand on the horn and gave the lady a quick blast to let her know we were coming up behind and for her to get out of the way.

Whoops – Yep – her again – ER II

The work as a beater is not easy. You walk for miles over the hills, moors, through rivers, across bogs. Half the time you are wet and cold and the rest of the time, on those rare sunny days in the Highlands of Scotland, you are boiling hot. We always started out very early in the morning as we had to be in place, up in the mountains, ready to start the first drive before their Lordships arrived.

We were supervised by one of the Queen Mum's Gillies or Gamekeepers and they were not shy of shouting down the line some rather explicit instructions to stay in line, or speed up, or slow down. This kind of language was quite ripe and it would echo across the moors and valleys. The Queen Mum and her lady guests did not arrive until lunch time when a large tent would be set out for them, so the language was always moderated after the ladies arrived. But – yes, another 'But'.

One day I was on one of the higher points on the hillside and the Head Gillie was quite a way down below me. He could not see that the Queen Mum and her lady guests had arrived early, and were getting ready for their lunch over by the butts. I think we had a few inexperienced beaters on that day and the Gillie was getting just a little upset that they were not keeping a good line. He was swearing like a trooper.
'Keep that fxxxing line straight'.
Fxxxing speed up on the right'.
Etc., etc.. The air was blue.

It was one of those still, quiet days with hardly a breath of wind.
You know the kind of days when you can hear a bird call five miles away.
His voice was echoing off the distant hills. Crystal clear.
As the echoes bounced back it just seemed to be a repeating string of Fxxxings

Hurried messages sent down the line to shut him up.
Funny – Nice memories.

Not all the Queen Mum's shooting guests were accomplished shots and some of them were downright dangerous. You see, as the line of beaters gets closer to the 'butts' the shooter (or 'guns' as they are called) are supposed to only shoot at the birds after they have passed through or over the butts. That way you don't go shooting, wounding or killing any of the poor peasant beaters. Grouse fly low and fast so as the beaters approach the line of guns there is real risk of being peppered with shot. The Gillie always shouted ahead when we were getting close, for their Lordships to only shoot at birds behind the line of butts. But there was one guest, and it was the same one every time, who obviously considered that peasant beaters were expendable, mere commoners, cannon fodder, and he would continue to shoot in our direction. We used to get a right old peppering from this idiot. He didn't seem to care.

Now I understood why they gave us those white flags to wave –

'Don't shoot! We surrender!'.

Last little bit of this story.

Over the years both at the Gillies ball and at the Cocktail Parties that the Queen Mum would hold for us at Birkhall, I got to know HRH Princess Anne quite well.

Don't go reading anything into this. There is no tabloid story here.

We agreed to write to each other while she was at Benenden School and I was to give her names of good films that she could request for their private cinema in Buckingham Palace.

I think I made a bit of a mess on my first suggestion which was 'Tom Jones'. That was quite a raunchy film in its day and I am sure that ER II would not have been amused.

HRH wrote to me quite regularly and small blue envelopes would arrive at school for me with a very small 'A' in the bottom left hand corner of the envelope. I would know who it was from. My return letters had to have a small 'TR' on the envelope to avoid them being opened by her security staff.

Her letters were really nice. Full of family news and very chatty. Just signed 'Anne'.

I did make one stupid mistake in one of my early letters to

her. I still cringe when I think about it. How wonderfully stupid we can be at that age.

In one of my early letters I mentioned that my birthday was coming up. Oh Lordy be! Why did I do that? Why did I even mention it?

HRH was kind enough to write back wishing me a happy birthday and that she was sorry she could not send a present but she was 'broke'. Lovely.

What in heaven's name did you expect Trevor?

"Hi my darling Trevor – It just happens that Mummy has a Rolls Royce that she doesn't use very much. I hope you enjoy it". Ha! Oh dear me – cringe.

I don't think I ever told anyone about this little pen-pal relationship but my parents and maybe my sisters knew about this as the postman would deliver Christmas Cards with 'Buckingham Palace' and 'ER II' stamped all over them.

These Christmas Cards were always sent by registered mail and I think our postman got quite a kick out of delivering them.

Sadly all these letters and Christmas cards were stolen many years later in one of my adventures in North Africa. Shame.

I always thought that I had kept that very secret but after about two or three years I started to get invitations to various upper crust cocktail parties around the Middlesbrough area. These were friends of my parents but normally I would never have been included. After all I was a dustbin man and everyone knew that story by now.

They gave away their ulterior motives early on.

'How's Anne'. '

'Tell us Trevor– How is the Royal family?'

etc..

I thought that was pretty sad. – I never bothered with these parties after that and always made excuses not to attend.

So – there we are – Extremes.

Balanced lad that young Trevor you know.

I wonder if Princess Anne ever knew that she was writing to a Dustbin Man.
  Hey, who cares – she was good at Latin, so was I.
  Anyone that good at Latin can't be all that bad!

I bet you all thought that this book was going to degenerate into a long list of sexual encounters and conquests didn't you? Well, I just proved you wrong.

Actually, my times up at Balmoral were very celibate. All the girls from St. Andrews were university students and I was still just a school kid, so there was not much chance for me there. I think I became quite enamoured with one of the girls that was one of the regulars but I am afraid that it was not reciprocated.
  The only girl up there who was about my age was Princess Anne and there was not much chance of me brushing up my snogging skills with her. Hey Ho.

# Last bit of schooling

By the age of about 19 my poor parents had spent enough money filling the coffers of Durham School so it was decided that I would have one more go to retake my 'A' Levels at a Polytechnic College in Middlesbrough. This was going to be just one year of concentrated effort and this was going to be my last chance.

Actually I quite enjoyed this year at 'Poly' and ended with a couple of 'A's and a General Paper which some people count but I am not quite sure why.

I should have taken Latin.

It was quite a fun time too as I met some interesting lads and lasses at the college, some of whom have remained friends to this day.

Surprisingly I was not aware of any of the nastiness that I had seen at public school. Might be a lesson there.

There was none of the stuffiness of boarding school and we were free at the weekends to do what we wanted. So it was fun and I was free again. I had my bike. I had a 'Jo' as a girlfriend and life seemed pretty good.

I did take quite a bit of 'ribbing' at this Poly. For some reason our female Biology teacher, who was one of those shy spinster types took a bit of a shine to me. She would actually come and sit down next to me and touch my hands – in front of everybody – and tell me what lovely hands I had. Lord only knows what was going on in her mind. I dread to think.

Jee Wiz – I could have died of embarrassment. The others would be sniggering away and I would get non stop ribbing from them – 'My, what lovely hands you have Trevor'.

# WHAT TO DO WHEN I GROW UP?

Back to the gist of this story. I think you have enough of the background by now.

The problem on the horizon of course was –'what was I going to be when I grow up?'

Medicine was out of the question. I had tried getting into BOAC / BEA at Hamble for pilot training and been turned down because I get hay fever. I had tried the Fleet Air Arm and got the same result so I was at a bit of a loss what to do. It was about this time that I went to that famous 'Careers Advisory Bureau' and got the 'Lighthouse Keeper' as a possible career path. Hey Ho – what to do ?

It's a bit of a bugger this business of 'Careers'. There you are at something like nineteen or twenty years old with not a clue what you want to do or what you can do. The hassle with this is that for some poor young lad just out of school, all you see is this rather depressing picture of a 'career' or earning existence that just goes on and on into the dim and distant future. I think that we are partially brainwashed to accept that a good job in banking, or accounting will put enough bread on the table and allow you to tick over without too many problems through to a comfortable retirement in a little village somewhere. Not exactly awe inspiring stuff and I was loath to step onto this treadmill as I saw no way of getting off it.

Now, where was I? Oh yes, back at the famous Careers Advisory Bureau and trying to figure out just exactly what a Lighthouse Keeper did. For some reason, maybe intuition, I decided that Lighthouse Keeping might not be the career path for me. I think that it must have been a couple of months after that that I started to clutch at straws and finally managed to get my little head around the fact that whatever I chose to do then need not be a career for life. So, Renwick – get off your backside and do something, anything, and maybe, just maybe, you might enjoy it if you give it a go.

Here comes an unlikely outcome. A great friend of mine, Don, had also managed to achieve similar levels of academic mediocrity and had gone into Hotel Management. There was a four year course at Leeds Polytech and on the face of it, it seemed quite interesting. So gird up your loins Trevor and go for it.

Which is what I did, and boy oh boy, did we have some fun.

In reality the course was so simple that it was boring. It sounded impressive "The Higher National Diploma in Hotel Keeping and Catering". There were no great challenges in the course but I did learn a few things. For some reason I managed to excel at Law and Accounting. That seemed a bit odd and out of character but that's what happened. I have no idea why I was good at these subjects as I didn't really enjoy them all that much. Maybe it was the intricacy of law or the basic underlying common sense of it that appealed to me or at least made it relatively easy for me to grasp.

Like the others on this course I became a fully qualified Chef which was part of the course. You have to be a bit sceptical about this as British Chefs do not really command worldwide respect. People do not really gasp in astonishment and awe if you proclaim yourself to be a British Chef. We did do a bit more than learn how to cook chips and fry eggs and we were supposed to follow the classic French – Escoffier methods. That sounds more impressive doesn't it? Not sure how important that was but I do enjoy having a bash at cooking sometimes and I suppose it is not a worthless qualification.

The course was one of those sandwich courses where you do a year out in the industry to get a bit more exposure and experience and that was quite interesting and also managed to equip me with some survival skills which I made use of a few years later.

I worked at the Leeds Infirmary, learning about hospital catering, then at a place in Bradford learning about industrial catering and then in a few hotels and good restaurants.

So all in all it was not three years wasted but I never really used these new skills to follow any career.

Actually, my time in Leeds was one long party. I did very little studying and the testosterone levels were rising very high. I cannot really say that I was bad but I was a bit naughty. I was certainly no worse than any of my buddies but we all did a lot of bed hopping. Girlfriends changed fast, even by the hour. Girlfriends were swapped on a regular basis. That makes it sound a bit bad but I am sure that if the girls were telling these stories they would say that they did the same and changed boyfriends on a regular basis. It was terrible when I think back on it, but those were the 60's. The days of freedom and free love. Flower Power, The Pill and the Beatles. Wonderful.

The birth control pills were just becoming available and that made a huge difference to the quality of our sexual adventures but it also increased the risk of venereal disease which was really quite scary for us back then. It all seems like peanuts now with the HIV and AIDS epidemics. You also had to be a bit careful with any of your partners who may have had ambitions to head for the altar so there was quite a long period when you continued to buy condoms, by the dozen, – just in case, you understand.

"Condoms should be used on every conceivable occasion"

I shared a flat in Leeds with my buddy Don and we had a wonderful time. We both had the same sense of humour and we both had little motorbikes and we really got around. I won't bother to expand any more on that one. I think you get the gist of it from the previous paragraphs.

In Leeds I must have been one of the poorest students in the whole town. It was a skilfully managed plot by my father. In those days you could get a government grant to attend college but unfortunately this was judged on a 'means test' which evaluated your parental income and awarded these college grants on this basis. Unfortunately, my parent's income meant that I did not get a penny so I had to rely on my father to fork out the necessary. This was where his old North of England cunning came in.

Before I headed off to Leeds he sat me down in the lounge at home and declared that we must work out a budget for my time at college. It might be worth pointing out that I had never been truly financially independent up to that point, so although I had a pretty good idea of how much a beer cost, I did not have a lot of experience in paying rent, buying food, and the slightly more essential elements in staying alive.

I walked into the trap like a lamb to the slaughter.

He ran through the various cost elements, such as food at three pounds per week, rent at four pounds per week, etc., and then came to the important bit – Entertainment. He made the suggestion that one pound per week should be sufficient. Ha, Ha!

I had not yet been to that famous American School on Negotiating Skills. Neither did I fully appreciate the day to day costs that I was about to incur.

Like an idiot – I agreed to these arrangements. What the crafty old bugger did not tell me was that this was fixed for my entire time at college at Leeds and was non negotiable. Damn it but I was poor. I used to walk into the pub in the evening and introduce myself.

"I'm Trevor and mine's a pint. Thanks"

The only way out was to work in the evenings and that was another useful lesson. Doing Hotel Management it was easy to get evening work in restaurants or at large functions so I managed to survive and what was good about working like this is that they fed you as well. Very useful lesson learnt which would help me out of a few tight binds a few years down the road.

So I learnt to be a waiter, a wine waiter, a commis chef, all kinds of jobs. Not exactly challenging but it served its purpose and I had some extra cash and food in my belly, so life was not too bad.

It was during my time at Leeds that I got together with some of the friends I had made while at that Poly Tech in Middlesbrough. Some of them had gone to Leeds to study dentistry and we were good buddies. They were all very keen water skiers so we used to go up to the Lake District and ski on Ullswater nearly every weekend. Now these lads were well off so I used to scrounge a lift with them in their sports cars and my contribution was to get permission from my parents for us to stay at the cottage from time to time as it was quite close to Ullswater. That was where that little cottage became the den of iniquity. Musical beds!

One summer the other lads had already gone up to Ullswater and were staying at a camp site on the edge of the lake so that they could catch the calm water really early in the morning. I was having to work as part of the sandwich course I was doing.

Eventually, I finished my stint at whatever hotel it was where I had been working in the cellars as a materials or stock clerk. Very lowly position way down in the depths of the hotel.

This was a wonderful summer and the others had all been skiing for a couple of weeks by the time I rocked up. There was lots of laughter as they were all tanned and looking super healthy and I looked like a white slug that had just crawled out of its hiding hole. Yuuk!

By the lake side there was the Old Church Country Club where we used to launch our boats and there was a very attractive young waitress working there that I took a shine to. Not so much in an amorous sense. More lustful I would have to admit. To me she was just super sexy and it only took a couple of days before we were spending the nights together. I would head off to the pub with the lads where they would do their best to chat up the lasses and as soon as we got back to the camp site I would walk over to her room at the Country Club and she would be waiting for me after her work. Bloody hell it was good. We were both just using each other I think and the sex was fantastic. Free. Uninhibited. Wonderful. And I was fit too!

Less of these tales of sexual prowess Renwick – Get on with the story.

That particular summer we were all trying to master the ski jump which we had on the lake. These ski jumps can be quite hairy to begin with as it is just a wooden ramp sticking out of the water and you have to hit it just right. The speed of the boat must be just right, the angle you hit the ramp at must be just right and the speed that you approach at must be just right. One little miscalculation and you can slap into the ramp or tumble off the edge or just bounce over it in a mass of flaying arms and legs. Shit – you can get hurt on that beast.

48

I had done some of this jumping the year before and I thought that I had mastered it. But not this year. Every time I tried I fell, or was pulled over it, or splatted into the side, went over head first. Bloody hell – I was getting hurt and going nowhere.

It was only years afterwards that one of the lads, who always did the driving when I was jumping, admitted that he had had his eye on this little waitress and had been trying to get something going before I got there and that I had muscled in on what he considered to be his catch. So he had taken his subtle revenge and every time I had approached the jump he had just edged the boat in closer or steered away at the vital moment. This was guaranteed to cause you to fall and I never twigged on. Trusting little soul.

Another amusing story about this jump was the antics that the fathers of two of the lads got up to. These men were both ex fighter pilots for the WWII so nobody could doubt their courage but it was amusing to watch these two adults plucking up their courage to try the jump. They would literally sit on the shore of the lake with a bottle of Scotch between them and when they considered that they had built up enough Dutch Courage they would demand to have a go at the jump. I don't think the Scotch and ski jumping are a good mix but they never got hurt. I suppose they were so relaxed they just bounced off the jump.

Lots of fun and lots of laughs.

Last funny story about Ullswater and it's another water skiing story. Do you remember those large kites that were towed behind speed boats to lift you into the air? These were not the fancy parasails they use now. They were just like the early hang gliders, the only difference being that you were attached to the speed boat by about 200 feet of rope and you were literally towed into the air.

We had heard about these and we ordered one from the USA. It arrived in a big cardboard box and we took it over to Ullswater to give it a try. The local television news channel somehow heard about this and as it was the first one in that part of the UK, they also arrived at the edge of the lake to record this daring event.

We eventually figured out how this kite went together and after a couple of hours of fitting tubes, nuts and bolts and the nylon fabric we were ready. We were all looking at each other, expecting someone to leap forward to volunteer to be the 'test pilot' but nobody did. It did not take long for us to realise that nobody had a clue how to fly this thing. All we knew was that you hung under this thing with a small wooden disc which you could rest your backside on. You obviously could not let go with either hand so we figured out that once you got going, if you wanted to go faster and higher you nodded your head and if you wanted to slow down and come lower you shook your head. That sounded simple enough so the next job was to choose the test pilot.

It wasn't a very windy day and our little speed boat was one of the those beautiful aluminium 'Albatross' boats. Not all that powerful but a nice little ski boat.

So no wind – not a lot of power and all the other lads were quite a bit bigger and heavier than I was.

Yes – you guessed it – Trevor was going to do his Biggles impressions after all.

I got under this kite, out in the water, and the boat pulled way to take up the slack in the line. At this point you need to be aware that a normal ski rope is only about 30 – 40 feet long. This bloody thing was 200 feet long or more. You also need to know that when you normally drive the boat you go at full throttle to begin with to get the skier on top of the water. Ha Ha. You can see this one coming can't you?

The TV news crew were filming away as the boat took up the slack. I gave them a nod when I was ready and the driver floored the accelerator.

Have you ever been in one of those very high rise office buildings where they have these super high speed lifts? Or how about that feeling you get shortly after take off in an aircraft where the pilot zooms skyward and you are pressed down into you seat.

Well it was pretty much the same. No gentle, gradual climb – I literally shot skywards like a cork out of a champagne bottle. I was scared stiff. The boat seemed like a little dot directly below my trembling legs. I was desperately shaking my head to get the driver to slow down.

Which he did immediately! You can just imagine this can't you. Oh boy!

Afterwards we learnt to accelerate slowly and slow down gradually.

I did not slow down gradually – I was at nearly 200 feet when all forward speed came to an end.

Weeeeeeeee – Splat.

Splash would have been the wrong word. It does not give the correct sound. Far too soft.

All of this was shown on the local news that night. It looked like a Charlie Chaplin film.

'Those magnificent men in their flying machines, they go up diddly up up and they go down diddly down down, etc..'

# OFF TO SPAIN AND CATALYSTS

Sometimes when you look back at your life you can identify one experience or an encounter with one person that altered or changed your life. But for that one encounter or that one experience you have to go out there so that it can happen.

I told my son time and time again that he could sit there and watch television all his life and nothing – absolutely nothing, was going to happen to him. I think he understood. I hope so.

I think that my life up to this point had still been somewhat sheltered. I had done quite few things but there was always that comfort zone of a good home life and nothing really too adventurous. I certainly could not say that I was living off my wits. All my friends were the same and it was a real eye opener and a breath of exciting fresh air to find Paula living out of, and in, a plastic bag in Spain. I think that she was a catalyst that enabled me to make some pretty drastic changes to my way of life in the not too distant future. She was exciting, she was independent, she was wild and she was a hair dresser from the East End of London.

Let me tell you the story.

There were five of us who water skied nearly every weekend summer and winter, all year round. We would even crack the ice on the edge of the lake to ski in the winter. Brave little souls. In about 1966 or 1967 Dave's father offered to lend us his 1948 Mk IV Bentley and the little Albatross ski boat to take down to Spain for an extended summer holiday and to enjoy skiing in the warmer waters of the Mediterranean for a change.

Pretty decent and trusting of him don't you think?

This was in the days when we had export currency restrictions in the UK and you were only allowed to take fifty pounds per person out of the country. We intended to be away for three months so you can see the problem. Running a Bentley and a boat with only fifty quid each was going to require some creative thinking and ideas.

So off we went.

The old Bentley was laden to the gunwales as was the boat. We had as much food and survival rations jammed on board as possible. The last item we had to get was a three month supply of condoms for five healthy lads – just in case, you understand.

As we were waiting for the ferry in Dover I was given the job of going to the chemist to buy them. I cannot actually remember how many it was that I bought but they came in a very big box and I do remember the look on the face of the poor girl who served me.

Now we were ready.

The trip down through France was uneventful and we timed it so that we could drive over the Pyrenees during the cool of the night to avoid overheating the old Bentley.

We did not have any firm plans where we were going as the whole idea of this extended holiday was to tour down the east coast of Spain until we found a good bay or area to ski in and then stay there for a while before moving on.

Our first stop was at Palamos which has a fairly nice sheltered bay. There was a good camp site close to the beach so we put up our two big army ridge-pole tents and set up base. We used one tent as a store and cooking area and the other tent was sleeping quarters for all of us. These tents were big – none of those flimsy modern things for us. It looked like something out of an old war movie and did cause a few laughs and comments from the other campers who were all equipped with the latest and greatest.

The skiing was good but you had to be up at dawn to catch the early morning calm water. It would then rough up a bit during the morning and by ten o'clock it was usually too rough to continue so we would just lie about, have lunch, take a siesta and wait for the water to calm back down in the evening. We would then ski again until it was too dark to see what we were doing. Then it would be clean up and shower time and off to the local tavern.

We did that pretty much every day for the full three months. Wonderful.

We had not been in Palamos for more than a week when one evening we saw two girls arrive at the camp site and set up close to us. When I say, 'set up', I do not mean pitch a tent. They merely plopped their back packs on the ground and lay down next to them. We were about to go into town so we did not take too much notice.

The next morning we could see that these two girls were sleeping in two plastic bags on the ground with their backpacks as pillows. Now that is interesting. Hardy souls those two.

When we came back from our early morning skiing the two girls were there and we went over and introduced ourselves and started chatting away.

I had never met anyone quite like Paula. I cannot remember what her friend's name was. They were quite amazing. They were both only about 19 years old and had been hitch hiking all around Europe for the last four months or so. They had been attacked and nearly raped in Yugoslavia and had all other kinds of adventures.

I was absolutely fascinated. Paula was not a hippy. She was a real free spirit. Nothing phased her and there were no timetables in her life. No mountains to climb All obstacles either collapsed before she got to them or they were merely stepped over in a cool, calm, easy going stride.

I was not in love with Paula. I was in awe of her. I had never met a girl with so much guts and so much modesty. Nothing was a big deal.

I am going to go on a bit about this as I think that it changed my whole outlook on life. Up to that point I was eventually going to conform to whatever the norm was in the UK. It had not worried me too much but I suddenly had my blinkers taken off. There were options, there were choices, and they were not difficult. There was a wonderful and interesting life outside British suburbia. You could be carefree, penniless and happy.

She was also bloody good looking and sexy as well, but I think you knew that was coming didn't you. So I moved out of the big ridge pole tent we used for sleeping and Paula and I moved into the store tent.

I enjoyed Paula's company. She was very, very special. Wild, wonderful, interesting.

Then disaster. We had been in Palamos long enough and it was time for us to move on.

It was also time for Paula to go into Barcelona to sell some blood. You see what I mean about her now ? She could get about £5 for a litre of blood and she did this a bit more often than she should have done. The hassle was of course that we did not know where we were going and where we would stop off at next so there was no way that Paula and her friend would know where we were or where we had gone to.

Sadly, we bid our farewells and Paula promised she would try to find us.

Next morning we packed up our tents. Loaded the old Bentley and hitched up the boat and set off south.

The Spanish coast is not just some little one day tour you know and that part of the coastline is just one village/town holiday resort after another, so I really thought that I would never see Paula again.

We continued South until we came to Sitges which seemed as if it could be quite good for skiing so we toured around until we found a good camp site by the beach. Out with the old army tents and we were back in business. Skiing, sun. laying around and then sorting out the best night life spots. Life was great but I missed Paula. Not in a 'lost love' way. I just thought that she was absolutely great.

Anyway, after we had been in Sitges for about five or six days we were all lazing around on the beach after the early morning ski runs when, who comes strolling down the beach?

Yep – Paula and friend. Actually, she said finding us was really quite easy. She had stopped at every village or town and had asked if anyone had seen five lads drive by in a Bentley towing a speed boat. I suppose we did stick out a bit.

Wonderful times and we managed to make our limited cash stretch out by giving the British barmaids and waitresses from the local bar free ski lessons in exchange for the odd plate of food. I was also a bit of a bad bugger. While everyone was up dancing I would pretend to be a waiter and I would pinch their half finished drinks off the tables! Ohh – Naughty!

They were all so drunk they never seemed to notice.

'Another round over here Jimmy!'

As you can imagine we were very tanned by this stage and we always went barefoot so we must have looked like a bunch of hippies. We certainly did not look 'English'.

One evening we were coming out of our favourite bar in Sitges and there was an elderly English couple sitting on a wall right in front of where we had parked the Bentley. The husband was wearing long trousers and had socks on but was wearing sandals. I think it is only the English who can wear socks and sandals. He was also licking an ice cream.

As we approached he leant to his wife and said, in quite a loud voice,

"Just look at this lot"

As Paula walked past them she turned and said,

'Look at which lot'. She said this in a phoney upper crust, plum in the mouth, accent which was difficult for her as she was from the East End!

As we all climbed into the Bentley, and there quite a few of us, Dave, who was in the driving seat, wound down his window and leant out.

'I suppose you are a damn tourist – are you sir' – Again in a really put on aristocratic pompous voice.

The poor man nearly fell over backwards but the wife got it and was roaring with laughter.

All good fun. You realise here that I am going to leave out a lot of tales about this holiday but I think that I have covered the essential bits.

So our long holiday went on and eventually we had to head back to the north of England and Paula and her friend headed back to London in order to earn enough money for another adventure next year.

I went back to college in Leeds and I used to hitch-hike down to London to see Paula as often as I could. It was fun and it was wild but it was not destined to last. We were not in love and so eventually we went our separate ways. But my eyes had been opened and life was suddenly full of possibilities. Thank you Paula.

I also have Paula and her friends to thank for never being tempted to 'get into drugs'. Some of the parties in London were a bit on the wild side and marijuana and LSD were quite common at some of these does. One evening we were at a party with a bunch of wild side rock musicians and their groupies and they were high as kites. They had put a row of coloured plastic clothes pegs on a washing line and were sitting there, totally spaced out, saying in phoney American accents,

'Oh man them colours, I'm swallowing them colours'.

I though that was quite pathetic so I was never tempted to join the junky crowd. Thank God.

# WHERE TO NOW

When I finished this long drawn out college course in Hotel Management I was pretty cheesed off. Paula had sown a seed or two in my head and the thought of working in hotels did not appeal to me one little bit.

The norm was to go straight from college into a large hotel chain or some other side of the catering industry but I put it off and I put it off.

Why should I go and do something that I really did not enjoy?

So I searched around and tried to find something else.

It did not come easily.

Firstly, I joined Securicor and worked as a night security guard. They gave me a little Escort van and a radio (I was 'Charlie Mike 101') and a police reject Alsatian and I would go around factories and warehouses during the night to make sure that nobody had stolen them. Not bad. I was out there on my own and I think that it suited me up to a point. It wasn't exactly stimulating but it was quite good fun. I also had to do a few daylight runs on Sunday as overtime to cover for some of the other guards.

One Sunday morning I was doing one of these daylight runs and I had to go into this large deserted factory in Hartlepool. It was one of my regular night runs but this was the first time I had gone there in daylight. No big deal. It was just a bunch of old buildings. I had to walk down between the buildings to a point at the far end where I would turn a key in my tape machine which I carried to prove that I had actually been there at such and such a time. If you see what I mean.

Anyway, as I am walking through these deserted buildings

I suddenly notice a bunch of guys up on the roofs ripping off the lead guttering.

"Hi guys – working overtime. Have a nice day. Bye. See you later"

Quick on his feet this Renwick lad.

Relaxed stroll back to my little Escort humming a soothing little tune.

"Headquarters from Charlie Mike 101 – There are a bunch of guys ripping lead off the roof at XXX".

Actually, it turned out that it was perfectly legitimate but it did have me wondering for a while.

I also lost my Alsatian out of the back doors of the van one night. I was going round a roundabout and my dog was jumping around in the back. He must have hit the door catch because the next minute he was running alongside me barking his head off.

'Hey Trev wait for me, wait for me'.

This job was going nowhere so I gave it up after about a year.

My next job was going even further nowhere. Doorman/ Bouncer at a run down casino in downtown Middlesbrough. I use the term 'casino' lightly. It was actually just a gambling club in a semi detached house in a very run down area of town. The other side of this semi detached house was a brothel and again not exactly at the higher end of the market I think. Not that I know much about brothels of course.

The girls at the 'casino' were nice and the girls next door were always friendly so it was an easy job. Not much money though. Sort of going nowhere fast.

I would not have been a good bouncer if such talents had ever been needed. I am not exactly the physical confrontational type. The only time I was ever asked to see someone off the premises I just asked him very politely if he would please leave, and he did. As quiet as a mouse. I am glad because he was about twice my size.

So Trevor lad we can't keep going like this. Decision time.

My reasoning told me that I should give hotels a try. After all I had spent four years doing that supposedly high power course, so why waste it?

"Give it a try Trev, you never know you might enjoy it"

"No you won't", said another voice but I didn't really have much choice, did I? So I did.

# HOTELS

I joined a group of hotels which were the upper market part of a chain owned by a large brewery, all four and five star stuff. The first hotel that I worked in for them was in Gosforth in Newcastle. I was to be the night assistant manager which is not exactly awe inspiring stuff. Basically, you just tally up all the cash, do a balance check on the NCR registers and do the cash banking and checks. You also have to deal with the odd request from customers in the middle of the night.

Now, in England in those days we tended to be just a little bit behind the rest of the world with regards to service quality in our hotels and unfortunately that was what I was used to. I had never been in an American hotel, a Hilton or Intercontinental so I was not exactly 'worldly' in the international sense of the word.

One evening an American lady guest called down at about 11.00 pm and asked for a face flannel to be sent up to her room. I knew what a face flannel was of course. I also knew that a face flannel was a personal item and you did not use other people's face flannels.

Whooops – I told her that she would have to buy her own face flannel the next time she was in a chemists shop or wherever you buy face flannels. Face flannels were personal items and she should have her own, etc., etc.. The poor general manager had to sort all this out the next morning. She was furious and she was absolutely right. I could cringe when I think about it now.

What else ? Oh yes – cars.

For the first time I was able to save a bit of money and I needed transport beyond my old motorbike. My first car was a very old Volkswagen Beetle. The very old ones with the small oval window in the back. I got it for the princely sum of £17 from a scrap yard with a spare engine thrown in. That old car did a lot of miles. I would rebuild one engine and have it on standby until the one in the car started to make funny noises and then I would swap them out and rebuild the older engine and so on. I got quite expert at that and could change these engines out in less than an hour. Hey, but there are only four bolts and a couple of cables. So that was my trusty steed. Not much power and the only way to turn the heating on was to climb out and stuff a rag into the holes where the air circulated out from the engine. The heating pipes along the sides of the car were so rotten with rust that I had to fix them by glass fibering in a series of cardboard tubes from the inside of toilet rolls. Don't scoff – it worked.

After working at this Hotel in Gosforth I was transferred up to Scotland and worked at a rather nice old hotel in Sterling. Nothing too exciting again. Got a new partner there and it was fun but her heart wasn't in it and neither was mine, so that was not going to last.

The only funny thing that happened there was when one of the guests died in the middle of the night and wasn't discovered until the next morning. By this time the area in reception was full of people checking out and the only way we could get this body out of the hotel to avoid this crowd was down in the lift. It was one of those very small lifts.

Only way round this was to get the funeral guys to take the coffin down, upright.

I was actually at reception when the lift doors opened to reveal these two guys from the funeral parlour jammed fast in the lift with this upright coffin between them.

I thought it was amusing but that might not be everyone's cup of tea.

Then on to another hotel in Dundee. This one was my favourite of the lot. It had a lovely restaurant and the people working there were quite a bunch of characters. I had a little cottage in the grounds all to myself as by this time I had risen to the dizzy highs of Food & Beverage Manager. Sounds good but doesn't really mean much, so don't get over impressed.

I probably learnt more about good food and wine and good service at that hotel than all the others put together. The manager was a nice person, he knew what he wanted and he knew what good food and good service was. That little restaurant used to win some quite prestigious prizes and was always fully booked. I used to spend a lot of time in the kitchen as this really was a hive of activity.

Have you ever seen or been in the kitchen of a really busy first class restaurant? It is amazing. It is a frantic, frenetic, noisy, hot, two to three hour period of apparent chaos. Orders are coming in all the time and every little part of the order has to be carefully prepared and timed to perfection so that at precisely the right moment the whole order has come together and is ready for a final check before being sent out to the restaurant. That final check was a job I did most of the time in the peak period. The person who does this is called an 'Aboyeur' – now I am not sure I have spelt that correctly but that's how I think it should be spelt in French. It really is the hub of a kitchen. It is the 'Aboyeur' who receives the orders from the waiters and who calls out the order to the various chefs working in the kitchen. He is the person that controls and coordinates the preparation of each order to ensure that it all comes together at the right time. He also does the final check that the food is as per the order, that it has been cooked correctly and that the presentation is good. See what I mean – A really important guy.

I had a fascinating girlfriend up in Dundee. She was drop dead gorgeous, she could play the piano like nobody I had ever met, she could play squash, she had a magnificent body and she was absolutely useless in bed.

I have never met anyone more useless! What a waste! Are you asleep dear?

Okay, so I leant quite a bit. I was saving a bit of money but I was not really a happy chappy.

On to the next Hotel – This one was in Aviemore and I thought that this might be a nice change as I had done some snow skiing when I was at school and here was my chance to brush up on that sport. By this time I had managed to blow up my old Volkswagen and I now had a beautiful Austin Healey 100/6 (1957) which I had managed to pick up for all of £160. I loved that car. It was like driving a tank but it had character, and that exhaust noise – Ecstasy!

I rebuilt that car as much as I could. It was not in bad condition when I got it but I just enjoyed fixing things up and still do.

Aviemore was okay. This time I managed to find a nice partner. Maggie. Boy oh boy, she was fun. She used to call my old Healey the 'Beastie' and we had a load of fun roaring around and skiing and touring. We went on holidays together and we were really quite well matched. Actually, of all my early girlfriends around that time I would have to say that Maggie was the most 'suitable' if you understand what I mean. We got on very well, we had lots of laughs, we enjoyed the same things and we had fun.

Unfortunately, or maybe fortunately, we ended up going our merry ways. I went off to Aberdeen to be assistant manager at an older hotel up there and Maggie was transferred to Edinburgh. We tried to keep it going for a while but working in hotels does not give you a lot of time off and the hours are really antisocial. So that was the end of that one but I do remember that relationship with fond memories. I hope everything worked out for Maggie. I am sure it did as she had the personality to conquer the world.

You must be getting bored with this. I am bored just writing it. We are getting nowhere and that is exactly what I thought back at this stage in my life. You can see the important bits shining through but there was nothing shining through at that point in my life. The things that made a difference or the people that you meet that make a difference seemed a long way from this hotel work. Not too many laughs either. I was rapidly approaching the time for a change and it had better be a good one.

So where next Trev lad? – Oh yes – now we are coming to the interesting bits.

Remember Paula and the catalyst. The person who opened my eyes to endless possibilities. Well, they were just about to happen again.

By chance I was sent down to Perth to one of the lower star rated hotels to act as manager while the resident boss took his summer leave. Nothing special about the hotel. It was a bit at the lower end of the market so there was not a lot for me to do except just hold the reins.

By this time I had a rather fancy TVR sports car as well as my old beloved Healey so I must have seemed a bit of a playboy – which of course is what I secretly was. A penniless playboy. These kinds of sports cars do have an influence in attracting the opposite sex so I really had no problem attracting the lasses as you can probably gather by now. But – and there is a but here, quite frankly most of the people I knew at that time were quite boring. I don't mean that in a nasty way. It is just that none of them had the spirit, that willingness or enthusiasm to try something new, something different and exciting.

It just so happened that there were two Australian girls working as waitresses in this hotel in Perth. They were doing the obligatory (for young Australians) year in Europe and working their way as they went. A job here, a job there, whenever the money was running short. This life style appealed to me. I had always been interested in exploring new places, new experiences and here were two young lasses, free as birds, doing whatever they wanted, whenever they wanted, and there was I stuck in this boring job and going nowhere.

One of the girls was 'Joanne' (you see I had the name right) and she was from Tambo in Western Queensland. She was a bundle of energy. Quite good looking with dark brown eyes and long dark brown hair. We started to spend quite a lot of time together and the relationship blossomed. I think that I was a bit of a safe haven for her. A chance for her to relax and be looked after. You have to be aware that when you are travelling as she was, you are really just 'bumming around'. You have next to no money and you are living hand to mouth, sometimes never knowing where your next meal is coming from. You certainly cannot afford to stay in hotels or eat in restaurants, so when you meet or bump into someone you like and who can look after you, take you out and roar around the country in a fancy car, it does have a certain appeal.

So this is what we did and I would take Joanne and her friend out for nice dinners and I took them down to the Lake District to stay at the 'cottage'. They loved this of course, but I think her friend got a bit tired of being the 'gooseberry'.

The more time I spend with Joanne the more I liked her. I don't know if I loved her. Maybe. I think that at the time I thought that I loved her, but looking back on it now, I am not so sure. She also seemed to be 'in love' and she told me so. She was incredibly affectionate and it seemed as if we really were in love but in hindsight I would have to say that it was more the circumstances that influenced this depth of the relationship.

Anyway, she was the 'reagent' that I needed. Paula had planted the seed some years before and it was Joanne that made me get off my butt and change my life.

One of those wonderful people who make a difference. One of those amazing people who can actually change the world around them.

Since those days, I have met quite a few of these shakers and movers but only because I let it happen. I would certainly not have met people like this if I had stayed in the hotel industry.

Joanne and I spent quite a few months together. I had moved to a hotel in Giffnock which is on the west side of Glasgow to work as assistant manager and we could now only spend our days off together. It was not ideal but we would spend every available minute together. Her friend was getting pretty pissed off by this time as their plan had been to tour around together and one girl cannot do that on her own. I had thrown a spanner in the works. Joanne finally agreed to hit the road again with her friend. So we parted swearing undying love and devotion to each other. Tears, hugs and kisses.

Joanne finished her touring and eventually it was time for her to fly back to Australia. Up to this point I had still not consciously realised that my life was just about to change. I wonder if I expected Joanne to stay in the UK with me and our life would continue as it had up to then. My blinkers had not quite come off yet you see.

The last straw was that hotel in Glasgow. Bloody hell I hated it. I was bored to tears. The manager was a crook and the customers were not what I was used to – Is that a nice way of putting it?

Before I close this part of the saga I must tell you about a really embarrassing thing that happened at that hotel. Do you remember my days as the doorman / bouncer at that club in Middlesbrough and the fact that I am not really 'physical' or 'confrontational', in the sense that I would hardly ever lay my hands on anyone? Well, unfortunately I did 'lay my hands' on someone while I was there, and it was definitely the wrong person!

I was doing my evening shift, keeping an eye on the restaurant and the kitchen when I got a call from the cocktail bar that two chaps were causing a bit of trouble. So off I went and sure enough there were these two guys sitting at the bar stools and swearing away like troopers – they tend to do that quite a lot around Glasgow. So I politely told them to behave themselves and cool it otherwise I would have to ask them to leave.

'Aye Jimmy – al rite'.

Off I went, but within twenty minutes I got another call from the bar to say that these two were at it again. This time they were still sitting on their bar stools but they were grabbing each other and swearing at the tops of their voices. The air was blue and the other quests and couples in the bar were looking distinctly uncomfortable.

What I did not see was the pair of crutches propped up against the end of the bar.

Yep – you guessed it. I grabbed one of these lads by the arm and pulled him off his stool with the intent of frog marching him off the premises. Whooops – he fell to the ground, his withered legs collapsing under him. Oh dear me. I could have died of embarrassment.

Okay –so where are we now? We have just spent about two to three years in a job that I hated. I have had very little fun and nearly everyone I have met was as boring as sin. Time to make a move. Decision time moon beam!

I had been phoning Joanne in Australia and I told her that I was going to come out to Australia. She seemed overjoyed. So that was it – decision made – as easy as that!

I sold my cars, as those were the only assets I had in the world, and after paying off what I still owed the bank I had enough money for a cheapy, cheapy ticket to Brisbane and two hundred pounds of spending money. That was it. – Lump sum total of my life to date.

My last great act of defiance before leaving, was to take my hotel working clothes which were the pin stripe trousers, black jackets, grey waistcoats, silver ties, put them on a tall metal coat stand in the middle of the hotel car park– pour paraffin over them and set light to them.

Now let's get out of here Trevor.

# AUSTRALIA

That was one long flight. I went out with Thai International with stops at Tehran to refuel, then on to Bangkok for another refuel. Then on to Singapore and the final leg to Sydney. We landed late in the evening and my domestic connection to Brisbane was not until the next morning. Not having any money to speak of, staying at an hotel was out of the question. So I just stayed in the airport and doss'd down on one of the seats and spent a very uncomfortable night trying to make sure that my suitcase was not stolen and try to catch a bit of kip at the same time. I was to do a lot more dossing down in the future but I was not used to it at this point.

Nowadays, we do these long haul flights every day, but back in 1972 they were awful. The planes were cramped and there was hardly room to swing a cat. I think that my flying time just to Sydney was something like 36 hours. It was also the first time I had done a long haul and it was the first time I had experienced jet lag. So when I eventually got to Brisbane I was dead on my feet and I must have looked a bit of a mess.

Be that as it may. Joanne was at the airport to meet me and it was super to see her again. Huge hugs, kisses and holding each other in case this might not be true. Great.

Joanne's parents were taking their annual break from the Outback and had rented a small house at Surfer's Paradise on the Gold Coast. Damn – but that was beautiful. This was a whole new world for me. I had just stepped through the 'looking glass'. Everything was new and exciting. The colour of the sea, the sky, the waves, the wind – absolutely everything was exciting and different. I walked, I swam, I ran, I hired a big learner's surfboard and made an idiot of myself. Fun. Fun. Fun.

Unfortunately, with Joanne's parents there, we were back to 'snogging' and sleeping in separate rooms but that was okay. I was so happy, free and excited that I really didn't mind too much. Actually, this sexual starvation went on for quite a long time as before long we were heading west, out to the property in Tambo and again to separate bedrooms. Hey Ho Trevor – You can live with this.

The drive back out to Western Queensland was also fascinating. As a kid you had seen the old 'Westerns' in the cinema with the stage coach hurtling along with clouds of dust trailing behind.

I had never been 'hurtling along with clouds of dust trailing behind'. It was all new. I was fascinated just to stare out of the car at the passing countryside and look behind to see these 'clouds of dust trailing behind'. It was great.

The road was mainly a dirt road as you have probably gathered and it was a fair old hike. Something like 800 kilometres which for a poor little lad from England was also quite amazing. Nowadays, in South Africa we drive over 1000 kms at a go and think nothing of it.

I had recently read the story of the Burk & Wills expedition across Australia so I was spell bound as I watched the country side gradually change as we went further west. The gum trees gave way to farm land, which gradually gave way to flat savannah cattle country.

Beautiful. The more arid and desolate the scenery became the more I liked it.

Joanne's parents were wonderful. They were kind and considerate but they must have wondered what I was up to. What were my intentions with their daughter? I don't really think I had any idea what my intentions were. I was living for the minute. Joanne also had two brothers and they were also good guys. One of them lived in Brisbane and the other had a business somewhere but they both came out to the property in Tambo quite often. They were all very good company.

Joanne and her father showed me around the area as well as an area nearby where there were some wonderful caves with Aborigine paintings on the walls. I was thrilled.

They also took me to stay at one of their friend's properties. Apparently this family was quite well known and Prince Charles had even stayed with them when he was in Aussie.

I didn't bother to mention that I knew his sister quite well.

Once I got my feet on the ground I realised that I would have to help out around the property. I could not just sit around waiting to be fed. So Joanne and I would saddle up the horses and go out to round up the cattle and move them from paddock to paddock.

This is called 'mustering' in Aussie. This was serious long duration riding. None of the bolt upright English riding style here. You were in the saddle literally from dawn to dusk with a short break around midday just to stretch your legs and to pick up some drink and food which was left on the trail at pre-arranged points. I really enjoyed this but it was hard work. I learnt to ride Aussie style in an Aussie saddle which is more like a Western Saddle. You sit down into the saddle and try to keep everything relaxed. That way is not so tiring. Actually, although you spend a long time in the saddle most of the time you are just walking along at the same pace as the cattle. So it is not long periods of trotting or cantering and if you stay relaxed it is not too exhausting. The only time you have to get a move on is when the cattle break out of the herd. Then you have to get them back as fast as you can or the whole herd starts breaking up with cattle going in all directions. Then you have your work cut out and you have to gallop fast through the bush to bring them back into the herd.

When I say that we were driving the cattle from paddock

to paddock I am talking about Australian Outback cattle farm paddocks not little paddocks you find in the UK. These Australian paddocks are thousands of acres each. They are huge.

We would ride out early in the morning and go into whatever paddock the cattle had to be moved from. This stage of 'mustering' can be done at speed because you have to go around that whole paddock to find out where the cattle are and then start them off in the right direction. It is only when you have all the cattle together that you can slow it down to a nice walking pace. Then you would gently guide them to the gate and then 'drive' them along the trail to their new paddock . All these moves are to keep the grazing in each paddock fresh and to 'rest' a paddock in case it gets overgrazed. As this is way out in Western Queensland the grasslands are not lush green pastures, they are dried up savannah grasslands and this does not support large numbers of cattle.

Okay – interesting and fun but very hard work.

One of the most interesting and exciting experiences I had while on this property in Tambo was 'breaking in' two young horses. The horses are allowed to roam free around the property and obviously, from time to time there are some foals born.

There were these two young fillies or colts (I am never sure when a filly becomes a mare or a colt becomes a stallion) who must have been about one year old. Maybe a bit more – I really do not know – but they were young.

Anyway, Joanne and I rounded them up and drove them to the main fenced corral area. Joanne had obviously done this many times before but it was all new to me. We were riding these two young horses in four days. Now I know that our Texan friends will say that you can be riding a horse within 30 minutes by literally breaking him but we used the long, slow method. Very similar to the 'Horse Whisperer' way of treating horses.

You spend all the first day just talking softly to the horse – I mean all day – non stop. This then progresses to touching, stroking and talking. It was wonderful to see the way that the horses' confidence and trust gradually builds. Then it was putting blankets on their backs and continuing the touching stroking and talking. The last couple of days we were at the stage of putting a saddle loosely on their backs and continuing the same touching, stroking and talking. Then Bingo – you are up in the saddle.

What stays in my mind was the amazing bond that the horse builds up with you. When we first rounded them up and drove them into the corral they were scared and jittery and did not want you anywhere near them. By the end of four days they would run to the edge of the corral to greet us when we came down in the morning, tossing their heads and whineying in pleasure. Amazing.

I also managed to help Joanne's father with some of his vehicles. I had done most of my own mechanics work with my Beetle as well as the Healey and the TVR so I knew a bit. Not a lot, but a bit.

The property had a very old Series II (might even have been a Series 1) Land Rover which was just sitting in the barn on flat tires. I asked what was wrong with it and he told me that the front wheel bearings and brakes were gone and that he did not have the time to get it fixed and he would have to take it all the way into Tambo which was about 60 kilometres of rough farm track. So I volunteered and got it all apart and sorted out what was needed. We ordered the parts from the garage in Tambo and in about a couple of weeks we had this old lady up and running again.

The other vehicle sitting in the barn was the old world

famous Grey Ferguson Tractor – circa 1955. You must have seen these. You started them on petrol and then switched to paraffin. Just about every farm in the world had one.

Anyway this one had an undefined engine problem so I stripped it down, cylinder head off, sump off, pistons out, the whole nine yards. It took me about four weeks to get all the parts needed but then it was back together and running like a little sewing machine. I was quite pleased with myself.

What else? Oh yes, Joanne's dad had a Browning Automatic 12 gauge shotgun that was kaput. Something about the auto mechanism. So I sat there in the evenings with this gun in bits on the table until I found out what was wrong and fixed it. I cannot remember what it was that was causing the problem but it was a simple thing. Praise was heaped on me.

'Wow – that gun has not worked for years – well done Trev'.

I let the praises come. I was not going to let on that it had been simple to fix.

During the weekends on the property, when we were not mustering cattle, Joanne and I and sometimes one of her brothers would go out pig shooting. That part of Queensland is plagued with wild black pigs. They are not like the smaller wild boar but are big and black and the boars have some ferocious tusks. Most of the time we would drive out on the Land Rover until we found some pigs and then would try to bring them down with shots fired from the back of the open Land Rover. I was standing in the back of the Land Rover one day and we had come up to this group of pigs. Joanne's brother was driving and he had stopped to allow me to take aim and get a good shot. As I was about to shoot, he decided that he could get closer and without any warning he let the clutch out and set off. I went over the back of the Land Rover with the gun still held into my shoulder and landed flat on my back with the gun pointing to the heavens.

This could really have been bloody dangerous as the gun was loaded, cocked and my finger must have been on the trigger or near it. I think that even as I was going arse over apex off the back of the Land Rover I realised that it was going to be far more dangerous to release the gun and try to break my fall so I just held onto the gun and went over the back still in a perfect shooting stance. Whack into the ground, which is pretty hard stuff in Western Queensland.

What I haven't mentioned yet is that we were shooting these wild pigs with a little, .22 single shot, bolt action rifle. Not exactly the ideal gun for beasts like this and in hindsight it was a bit cruel as a little .22 does not really have the punch required for a clean kill. There was an old Lee Enfield 303 at the property but we had no bullets for it and it was in a very sad state, so it was the .22 or nothing.

The other thing about this was that as you could rarely get a kill with a single shot you had to chase the wounded animal on foot to finish it off as quickly as possible. That can make you pucker up a bit. Chasing a wild pig, who has some pretty impressive armament himself, on foot with a little .22 does kind of put you 'in harms way' as the Americans say. A wounded pig is usually not in the best humour and can still run at a pretty good pace so you do have to take a bit of care.

Joanne was amazing at this. We would normally try for a shot to the chest first as this was the best way to slow them down and was about the only vulnerable place to stand a chance of bringing them down with one shot. A head shot with a little .22 at 40 to 50 yards was not really going to work.

After we chased the pig on foot it would usually be on the ground if the first shot was any good. Joanne had a little .22 revolver and she would run in at the wounded pig, jump over the top of it and as she jumped she would fire a shot into the back of its head to finish the poor beast off.

I know that this will not be everyone's cup of tea but it is part of the tale so you will have to live with it.

After about six months on this property I had to get on and make a move. I liked Australia but I could not stay as a guest on the property forever so it was time to explore the country and to try to find some work to top up my meagre resources.

The relationship with Joanne had been good and I think we were a bit loath to let it go. We had never recovered the passions that we had while she was in the UK and I think that both of us realised that this was not going to work. I was also not much of a 'catch' either now that I had given everything up. I was a penniless English drifter with no job. Not exactly a good prospect in the marriage stakes.

Just before I left we had our one and only really intimate moment in the sheep shearing shed. Wonderful. I think we were both trying to recapture something that was already lost and gone. Hey Ho

Before I forget – one funny little story about Tambo.

Tambo is a tiny little town and it is right in the middle of cattle country as you have probably gathered. There was a tiny pub in town – the usual Aussie Outback pub – white tiles all the way to the ceiling so that they could hose the whole place down at the end of the day. No women allowed in either.

One day I had gone into town with Joanne's brother and we had gone off to the pub. You might have already twigged on that I like a good laugh and I am not shy of teasing people or making fun. So there I was in this pub. It was early evening and the place was busy with farm hands who had come in to wet their whistles. They were all friends of Joanne's brother so there was a lot of teasing about pommy bastards, etc..

There was a lull in the din inside the pub so I shouted out:

'Gentlemen, please raise your glasses – The Queen'

Ha ha – out of the door I went – head over heals on the pavement. But it was all done in good humour and I wasn't hurt. Stand up, brush down and back into the bar to the cheers and laughter of the lads inside.

# BURK & WILLS

I left Tambo with mixed feelings. Joanne and I had rekindled something in the sheep shearing shed but I could not stay there forever.

I got a lift with Joanne's brother who was leaving for Brisbane and he was kind enough to let me stay at his place while I tried to find work. Actually it only took me a few days.

There was a firm called Petty Ray that was advertising for crews for some seismic work out in the Simpson Desert and into the Channel Country (Cooper's Creek area) down in South Western Queensland. The pay was good, the living conditions were going to be rough and it was exactly the kind of adventure I was looking for. I signed up and was given a train ticket which would take me way out west to a place called Quilpie.

The train was slow – I mean slow. It took all of two days to get out to Quilpie. It stopped at every farm and property on the way to deliver newspapers or mail. The track undulated over every little contour but it was fascinating.

There were a few of us on that train going out to the seismic work and we were all picked up from Quilpe and taken way out west in the back of a lorry. I don't know exactly how far we went but it was a long way.

Jobs like these in the middle of nowhere do not appeal to everyone. But they do appeal to anyone who is running from the police. We had a lot of people running from the police in that crew. I would not say that they were exactly harmless but I sure would not like to have been on the wrong side of them. For some reason they seemed to accept this Pommy Bastard with the posh accent.

We lived in tents and there was a trailer that served as a kitchen. There was a communal shower trailer and that was it. Really basic living

It was fun and interesting. I had never been in a desert before and we went a fair way into the Simpson with its bright red sand. I loved this desert. It had a very special beauty.

What amazed me was not just the beauty but this desert was alive. All it took was a good downpour of rain and the whole desert came alive. This obviously did not happen very often but it did happen while I was there and the transformation was astounding. The whole desert was covered in a carpet of flowers two days after the rains. It was spectacular.

This part of Australia also has a lot of snakes and we used to see at least ten or more snakes every day. Some were nasties and some were harmless but I never learnt the difference and always took the cowards way out and treated every one of them as being the most deadly variety possible. What did I care – a snake was a bloody snake and I was going nowhere near any of them, harmless or not. One day one of the lads chased after what he thought was a harmless carpet snake and caught it in his bare hands. He was proudly waving this beast above his head when one of the more experienced lads came up to him and, trying not to panic him, gently told him the throw the snake as far away from him as possible, and quickly. I think the message got through. The poor lad turned pale and he heaved, what was quite a large snake, away into some scrub. Apparently, this was some super deadly snake that looked just like the harmless carpet snake. On the other hand the lads might just have been having a bit of fun and scaring this poor chap.

Another funny incident with snakes was when we had the storm that transformed the desert into the carpet of flowers.

We always pitched the living camp on a piece of high ground just in case. There was no need to pitch it on top of a hill but care was always taken that we did not camp in any hollows that might get flooded. When those rains came it was really quite major and the ground all around the camp was under water. Snakes do not generally like being under water and tend to head for higher ground. You remember all those guys running or hiding from the police ? Well, quite a lot of them were carrying or had firearms and mostly these were pistols. As the snakes came through the camp, and there were a lot of them, these idiots were standing on the camp beds trying to shoot the snakes as they came through the tents. Made a hell of a mess of the groundsheets but I don't think they hit a single snake.

The camp was alive with people shouting, yelling, swearing and the sounds of shots going off everywhere and then more swearing. It was chaos and a lot of laughs when it was all over.

The other thing that happens when it rains in that part of the world is that the bowls of 'bulldust' turn into a slimy, slippery mud. I do not know what is in 'bulldust' but I think that Shell or Castrol should investigate. It is worse than trying to drive on ice. The damn stuff is like liquid Teflon. Whatever is in it must be worth a fortune as a lubricant and nothing can drive through that stuff. Go for it Shell and if you find the secret ingredient, I want a cut.

Working on a seismic line at the level that I was employed at, which was the lowest of the low, a 'Juggy', involved walking. Lots of it – all day. Basically what you are doing is to lay out strings of ground microphones or 'Geophones'. These are connected up to listen to, and record, the echoes of sound waves that are bounced off the underlying rock structures. That way you can map the underground structures and it gives you a pretty good idea of where you might find oil or gas.

The sound waves used to be generated by drilling shallow holes and then setting off sticks of dynamite. Boom –echo, echo, echo.

The crew that I was with used a more modern method. They had this big Kenworth truck that had a huge weight on a pulley system on the back of it. The weight would be pulled up until it was about six feet off the ground and then it was released. Thump more than bang but it did the same thing. Nowadays they have a similar system but they are called thumper trucks. They lower a flat plate onto the ground and hit it with an air hammer.

We 'juggies' were the team that walked ahead of this thumper truck laying out the microphones. Good healthy work. The only hassle with this was that the lines had to be dead straight. You could not go round things or obstacles – you either had to go through them over them or under them but always in a dead straight line. This was okay up in the sandy part of the desert but the trucks did have a bit of a hassle. It was really interesting for us when we got down into the Channel Country which was way further south. There we had to wade across rivers and gullies, slipping and sliding through thick grey mud.

I did this for about four months, non stop. I liked the work. It was technically interesting if you took the trouble to try to find out how it all worked. It was healthy. It was basic. It was fun and I was exploring places where very few people had ever been. In fact we ended up right next to the base camp of Burk & Wills where they died after their historic overland expedition to the Gulf of Carpentaria. Fascinating.

I really had a job understanding why they had died there. The book on their expedition says that they died of hunger but all the creeks in that Channel Country are full of fresh water crayfish, turtles and all kinds of wildlife can be found around the creeks. I suppose that the creeks could have been dried out, but from what I saw, you should have been able to live off the land quite comfortably for a long, long time.

The other funny thing that I did not learn until many years later was that this company Petty Ray was later bought by Halliburton who I have been working with for the last 29 years. But that is still way down the line, so let's get on with the story.

Petty Ray asked me to come as part of the team to Western Australia as they had some other seismic lines to run there but I turned the offer down. I now had a pocket full of money and wanted to enjoy myself for a while. Actually, I think that I had more 'disposable' money than at any time in my life and I was going to use it wisely and explore and have fun.

Petty Ray had an aircraft for this last bit of work in the Channel County and we had built a dirt landing strip next to the camp. The plane was one of those Beechcraft twin engined things with about six seats. I was one of the last to leave the camp and we went over to put our meagre possessions onto the plane. The pilot was a woman and she was on her own.

Plane loaded, doors closed and it was time to go. The landing strip we had built was quite short so the pilot had to give it a 'bit of welly' to get airborne. No problems. Off we went.

Our first stop was going to be Charleville. I was going to get off there and head back to Tambo. The others were going on to Brisbane. As we were approaching Charleville at about 10,000 feet there was a huge tropical storm head of us. You could see it as clear as day. A great big black column about five or six miles wide right in front of us.

Charleville was on the other side of this storm.

Hey Ho – Here we go!

I don't know why but this pilot decided to go straight through this storm. She could have gone round it, but no – straight into it we went. Well, I have never been so bloody scared in all my life. I could also see that the pilot realised she had misjudged this one. Her hands were gripping the controls as they bucked and jerked around. The bloody plane was doing somersaults. Stuff was flying around in the cabin. The guy behind me was vomiting all over the place. I thought we were dead – I think the pilot thought that as well but she never let on. The whole thing probably lasted no more than 4 or 5 minutes but it felt like a lifetime.

But – I was meant to live another day so we got through and landed at Charleville.

# Playing Time

As soon as I got off that flight from hell I called Joanne up in Tambo thinking that we might be able to pick up where we left off – in the sheep shearing shed. Her father answered the phone and told me that Joanne and her brothers were at a local farmers dinner dance down at – guess where – Charleville. – Umm, this could be interesting.

I went to the local hotel and found out that, sure enough, there was a dinner dance being held there that night. So I booked myself a room and settled down to wait. I was not exactly kitted out to attend a dinner dance – torn off blue jeans and some worn out shorts.

You need to understand that by this stage I had been out in the middle of nowhere for four months and had not spoken to Joanne or had any communications at all for that time. I guess it was a bit naïve of me to think that she was just sitting around waiting for this penniless Pommy to return and sweep her off her feet. Neither would it be reasonable to think that she was going to the major dinner dance of the year on her own and just sit in a corner and pine. Joanne was not the kind of girl to leave the grass growing under her feet.

Sure enough at about five o'clock there she was – with her partner for the evening. She was obviously very surprised to see me and seemed genuinely pleased but the reality of the situation was that it was over. Her partner for the evening turned into her partner for the night. I got a lift with her and her brothers back up to Tambo the next morning but it was really only to say goodbye and to thank them for their hospitality.

It had been a great experience and I had enjoyed every minute of it. Joanne's father gave me a very glowing reference to help me on my way. These little one page references are very important when you are 'bumming' around.

So I went into Tambo and climbed on a bus and headed for Brisbane. Joannne's younger brother was back in Brisbane and, since we got on well together, he offered to let me stay there for a while to let me get my feet on the ground. I stayed there a few days and it was just party after party. Again I won't go into details as some friends who have already read the first part of this book have accused me of pornography and another has told me that it was getting a bit 'steamy' so I will not elaborate on this little episode. I will hint at it. I was very fit, very healthy, tanned and looking good and I had been out in the middle of nowhere for over four months without female company. Not Guinness Book of Records, but it must have been close.

Okay Trev lad – that's enough.

Last laugh in Brisbane before we move on.

I did toy with a job while I was in Brisbane. They were advertising for actors and male models in the local newspaper. I was just vain enough to think I might be able to make some good money out of this. The interview was very strange. It was in a very pokey office and there was a couple of rather shady looking characters there, sitting behind a desk. The interview got stranger and stranger as they first asked me to take off my shirt then my trousers, – hey what's going on here! But they were advertising for male models so maybe they needed to check my legs out. Their last request had them nailed. Yes, they did want actors but not for the kind of films that I had in mind. Definitely not going to be doing TV commercials selling soap powder. So – If you ever see any of those triple X-Rated movies that came out of Australia in about 1972 and you see someone that looks like me – It isn't – I did not take the job – I promise.

# EXPLORING

Now that I had a bit of money in my pocket I decided to just hit the road and explore the Barrier Reef and the Queensland coast to the north. I bought a nice backpack and sleeping bag as I had been living out of a small suitcase up to that time. I did not bother with a tent but I did have a plastic sheet which I could use as a bivouac, if needed. Hitch-hiking was relatively easy back then and I had no problems making my way up the coast stopping here and there, wherever I wanted and whenever I wanted. It was beautiful. The hassle is that there are so many islands to choose from it is difficult to decide which ones to explore. Back in those days the islands were still undeveloped and only a few of them had water or the basics that would allow you to stay over for a few days. I did not spend long on each island as there was a lot to see.

As you hitch hike around you bump into the same people time and time again. I suppose that this is logical. You are heading in the same direction. You can spend hours by the roadside trying to catch a lift and the places to see and visit, and stay at, tend to be the same for all of us. Sometimes I would go out to an island and see people that I had bumped into ten days before and other times I would stay on an island where there was hardly anybody.

I am not sure which I preferred. Being with a small group who sort of knew each other, or being on my own knowing nobody. There are advantages for both.

Most of the islands had designated areas where you can camp and most of these were very primitive which suited me fine. I did not bother with any bivy or cover. I would just lay out my sleeping bag snuggle up and sleep. I loved it.

I remember the island of Great Keppel impressed me quite a lot. I bought a ticket on one of the small tourist boats that take you out to the islands. They were great fun. Very basic and small. They used to hang a net out to the side of the boat so that you could climb down and lie in this net with the sea washing over you as the boat chugged along. There were dolphins and turtles and the water was crystal clear turquoise blue. Idyllic. There was a small area on the north west corner of Gt. Keppel where hitch hikers and campers could stay but it was pretty much deserted. The island was one of the bigger ones and it was super to walk into the small hills and look down on the beautiful bays. There was one small hotel on the island about one mile up the beach and it was lovely to walk up there as the sun was setting and relax and have a beer. Life seemed pretty good.

Another island that sticks in my mind was Magnetic Island, so named by Captain Cook when his compass went haywire when he anchored off it. This was not one of the white sand barrier reef coral islands. It was a jumbled heap of very large rounded boulders with small sandy bays scattered around the coast line. Quite beautiful in its own way, but different. There was no camp site there but if you walked about 2 miles away from the boat jetty you came across this lovely isolated beach to the north west of the island. That's where I headed for and found about four other hikers there that I had met before, who also had the same idea. These other hikers were better equipped than I was and they had snorkels and masks and they were a good bunch so we would spend the days together lazing around and swimming and snorkelling. Diving after turtles and trying to grab hold of them for a tow through the water. I have seen that being done in the current flood of nature programmes and it looks easy, doesn't it? Believe me it is not. The whole time there was magic. This group had set up their own little camp site above the high tide level but I decided to camp away from them. I found a nice cave up on the rocky slope above the beach and installed myself there. I stayed on Magnetic Island for at least two or three weeks, living in my little cave. It was nice. I would walk over to the landing jetty area once in a while for something to eat and sometimes spoil myself with a beer.

It was on this trip that I learned how to make my pennies stretch as far as possible. I worked out that if I ate one Australian hamburger and had one glass of milk per day that would be enough to keep me in reasonable shape. The Aussie hamburger is quite a beast by the way. Meat, bread, onions, tomatoes, lettuce. A meal in itself. So that's what I lived on. I even used sand to clean my teeth instead of toothpaste. – Hey -toothpaste is expensive!

I ended up rescuing a guy one day. I was down at the landing jetty one morning when a boat came in. It was not one of the tourist boats but was quite a large privately owned motor boat. As it approached the jetty it was obvious that one of the passengers was just going to be dropped off, so the boat did not manoeuvre to tie up but just came alongside, and held its position on its engines. The passenger was on deck and as the boat came alongside the jetty he jumped – and missed! He fell between the boat and the jetty and this was bloody dangerous. There was a ladder down the side of the jetty and I scrambled down this, got hold of the poor bugger and pulled him through the pilings away from the boat. We were both now in the water but safely behind the pilings. The boat pulled away so we climbed out from under the jetty and I helped this chap up the step ladder. Waves, thumbs up. All okay.

Then the S.O.B. just walked off without one word of thanks. Not even an offer to buy me a hamburger. There I was dripping wet, hungry and pissed off.

Cairns impressed me as well. It was getting quite tropical up there and the white coral sand, blue seas and palm trees made it seem a long, long way from Middlesbrough and North Yorkshire.

I liked Cairns. It was a busy little place, full of energy, bright and cheerful. Cairns is really the end of the tourist line (or it was then ). If you go further north you are into some really rough country up on the Cape York Peninsular. The roads are bad and it is very isolated. I don't mind living on my own and doing my own thing but to hitch hike any further north would have been stupid.

So I pondered on it a while and decided that if I was going to stay up in that area for a while I had better get a job and top up my liquidity. After all I had been travelling up the east coast for about three months by now and although I still had money left I may as well earn some while I explored the area.

So I went into the local jobs offices and searched around and before long I had an offer to work in a hotel up in Gove (Nhulunbuy) which is in the Aborigine Reserve of Arnhemland, way up on the west side of the Gulf of Carpentaria. The hotel was a little 3 star place called the Walkabout Hotel and they were offering to fly me up there to work as a night porter, which suited me fine. So off I went, not a care in the world and everything looking rosy.

# Arnhemland

This was really interesting. This was different. I was fascinated.

The hotel was nice, the work was easy and I had all day to do whatever I wanted once I had finished my work in the early morning and had a short sleep. The other people working there were also interesting. There was one chap who travelled all over the Northern Territories hunting buffalo with a bow and arrow. Now that is pushing your luck.

Another older couple were working to save enough for another sailing trip. They owned a small yacht somewhere and would go on some pretty adventurous trips in this boat until they ran out of money then they would catch some work, any work, wherever they were at the time until they were ready to take off again. Wonderful.

There were some nice lasses working there as well and before long I had teamed up with one of them as it suited us both. No pressures, no long terms plans or ambitions. Comfortable. She had a small 150cc scrambling bike and I would borrow that during the day and take off into the bush.

If you have not been in the Northern Territories before, you need to be advised that riding through the bush on a motorbike does have its risks. After all, this is not some cosy little suburb in England's Green & Pleasant Land, this is outback and there are some beasties out there and they are quite big.

I have still not seen spiders bigger than I saw there. They don't just have little webs between the branches of a bush or plant. They have webs strung between the trees! Not just little fine gossamer webs. These are ruddy great bungee cord webs – and the spider hangs right in the middle waiting for something like a water buffalo to walk into their trap. They are bloody huge. Now when you are riding through the bush on a motorbike it is usually too late by the time you see one of these monster webs across your track. Do you remember my old canoeing coach that used to say that 'Panic is fear of the unknown – therefore we are going to get to know the unknown'. Well, as far as these spiders are concerned they can stay 'unknown'. I had one land on my face. Well, actually he did not land on my face, I drove into him and my face collided with him. The damn thing was bigger than my hand and it was ones of those big, fat, hairy things. On a motorbike you do have a problem at this stage, as you cannot just let go of the handlebars to brush the beast off. The only thing to do is to stop as quickly as you can and then get rid of the beast. By this time panic is very close to the surface. Ahhhhhh!

Another time one landed on my chest, Ahhhhh!

Next scare, a huge, black, wild, water buffalo. These animals do not like being disturbed. They have a short temper and run on a short fuse. Round the corner I came and there was this mountain of black muscle and evil looking horns, just standing there. Oh bloody hell – get me out of here!

Arnhemland is a huge Aborigine reserve, or homeland I suppose. Not quite sure what the right name for it is. It stretches from just east of Darwin all the way to the Gulf of Carpentaria. The government had put up some breeze blocks type of houses for the Aborigines in Nhulunbuy but most of the Aborigines were far too intelligent to use them or even to see the need for them. Aborigines generally, tend to have a very bad reputation in Australia for being lazy, drunk and just slumming it on the outskirts of the major towns. I never saw this and I got to know some of the Aborigines in Nhulunbuy quite well. I found them fascinating. They were there because they wanted to be there. They had kept to their old traditions and were fully aware of their options and had chosen to live in the traditional Aborigine way. Yes – a few of them drank too much in the hotel bar but, by and large, I thought that they were wonderful. They taught me how to play the didgeridoo and tried to teach me how to hunt. They were absolute masters at hunting and living off the land. My poor little brain still hadn't twigged on to the fact that they had this life sussed out.

On one of my days off duty they invited me to go fishing with them. They said that there was a nice cove about 15 kilometres up the coast and that it was good hunting there. Of course I jumped at the chance and as I had the use of a four wheel drive vehicle I offered to give them a lift the next morning. They laughed. Aborigines laugh at us a lot by the way. They declined the offer of a lift saying that they would get there faster on foot. The track out to that area was not that bad so I could not see how they could get there faster than I could, so we had a little bet. The next morning we set off at dawn and I went off in the 4x4 and they went off on foot.

They are mainly tall and skinny – a bit like those Kenyan marathon runners. They can run all day long. Lopping along with an easy relaxed gait. They can also run in a straight line or as near as damn it and I was having to take the twists and turns as I drove along the track.

Well you know the answer don't you? There they were already set up in the cove by the time I got there.

We talked about why they didn't work at the local bauxite mines to earn money. They said,

'What do we want money for Trevor?'

'Well maybe you could buy a 4X4 with the money'

'What do we want a 4X4 for Trevor?'

You see, I still didn't get it. --- They did.

Watching them fishing was quite amazing. They had long spears with several sharp barbed points at the business end. They also use the Woomera which is the throwing stick. Sort

94

of an extension to your arm that allows you to throw the spear with more force. They would walk along the waters edge, but I think 'walk' is not the right word here. If you or I tried this we would splash and splodge through the water. They 'floated'. There was not a sound. Not a splash and hardly a ripple. The poor fish never heard them coming.

Also, their reactions were something I had never seen before and I have never seen it since. They were like lightning. It was almost as if they knew something was going to happen before it did.

I don't know if you have ever walked along a tropical beach with the waves curling in to the shore and suddenly you catch sight of the silhouette or shadow of a fish in the clear water of the wave.

'Hey – did you see that fish in the wave?' – Note the use of the past tense.

The Aborigine lads had already thrown the spear and got the fish – amazing.

Their art and culture was also spell binding. They use the stretched out bark of certain types of trees as their 'canvases' and they take care not to cut the whole ring of bark off a tree as this would kill it. The 'paint' is just chewed ochre of different tones of yellow, red and orange. Their brushes are the chewed short pieces of a certain twig that had a very fibrous stem. Beautiful throw away paint brushes growing all around. All materials readily available either lying on the ground or growing around you. Wonderful.

Also their paintings tell stories. They are not just pretty pictures.

I loved it. They had their lives well organised, full of songs and dance and the power of spirits.

I was actually honoured by them and went to one of their 'Corroborees' where they gave me an Aboriginal family name:

I am Trevor Witballah Unermurra – and I am very proud of it, even if I am not sure what it means.

So, all in all, a wonderful experience and one that I shall treasure all my life.

I stayed up in Gove for about four to five months and time passed nicely but it was time to move on.

# OFF TO NEW ZEALAND

While I was at this hotel in Gove I contacted Dave who was one of the old water skiing gang from England, as he had moved to Auckland with his wife and new baby and he was working as a doctor at one of the major hospitals in Auckland. I was ready to move on from Arnhemland and wanted to visit New Zealand and explore there for a while.

I must admit I was a bit cheeky as I sort of invited myself. At the time I didn't really think about it. Dave was an old friend and I just assumed that I would be welcome. Many years later when I had my own young family to look after I realised that this was a bit of an imposition. But hey – I did not intent to stay long.

So I bought myself a return cheapy ticket with a fixed return date. I gave myself six months to explore new Zealand and I thought this would be enough and actually it was.

Dave and his wife were kind but I stayed with them for a bit too long. I really needed to get a bit more of a cash cushion as the airline ticket had used up some of my reserves so my first task when I got there was to try to find another job. This was not as easy in Auckland as I had found it elsewhere and I was getting nowhere. Maybe I was getting fussy in my old age.

After about three weeks I still had not got any job or plan and I was overstaying my welcome so I just packed up my backpack and hit the road again.

First up through The Bay of Islands and on to the 90 mile Beach. Then backtrack down to Wellington and across to the South Island on a ferry. This was more like it. The South Island is spectacular. Hitching lifts seemed to be fairly easy and the New Zealanders I met were very nice and friendly. Down through the middle of the South Island, Mount Cook, McKenzie Country, Lake Tekapo and on down to Te Anau. It took me only about 4 weeks to get down to Te Anau and I had the usual fun of leapfrogging other hitch hikers. Wonderful fun with a bunch of real hippies in an old Bedford Bus done up in psychedelic colours – The bus that is, not the hippies Ha Ha! I think there was more horsepower inside the bus than under the bonnet.

I was amazed at the beauty of the South Island. The North Island is green and gentle and also beautiful but the South Island is just plain magnificent. I am sure you have all seen Lord of the Rings by now and that was all filmed in the South Island so you will have some idea of the splendour of the mountains and the scenery. Lake Tekapo is stunning. The backdrops are the high snow covered mountains and the foreground is this most beautiful bright turquoise lake. I had never seen anything like it in my life. Tekapo and Te Anau are two of the most popular spots to visit and all the hikers who had been leapfrogging each other down from the North Island seemed to gather there for a few days to soak up the scenery before moving on.

Te Anau is the gateway to Milford Sound so it also attracts a lot of visitors. When I say 'a lot of visitors' I am not talking about the European 'lots of visitors'. This is New Zealand and fairly sparsely populated and there certainly were not a lot of international tourists flooding into the country in those days. So although it was a tourist centre it was still a small quiet town.

By the time I got to Te Anau I was nearly out of money. I was down to my last $ 50.00 and it was time to stop and take stock and get some work. As Te Anau had a few hotels I started knocking on the doors and sure enough that same day I had secured a job as a wine waiter at the main hotel. It was investment time. I had to spend my last $50 on a pair of black trousers, a white shirt ( one only for the time being) and a black bow tie so that I could look the part. Wine waiters in patched jeans get some funny looks.

That evening I was away again – fed by the hotel, a few dollars in my pockets from tips and a roof over my head as they provided accommodation. Okay – wash the only white shirt I had every night, eventually invest in another after a few days and we were solvent again.

Wonderful – survival – easy.

The work was easy and I used my days off to explore. Hitching down to Milford Sound was probably the most impressive trip I made when I was there. That is really spectacular with these huge mountains rising straight out of the sea. The road to Milford Sound winds up through the mountains and then disappears straight into an imposing rock face. No fancy slip roads or signs (might be now of course) – just straight into a rough cut, unlined, unlit tunnel with spring water seeping through the roof and lying in puddles on the rough floor of the tunnel. Very dramatic. I wonder what it is like now.

Here we go – off on another relationship – OK boring – boring – boring.

There was a lovely lass from Austin, Texas, working at this hotel – Roxanne. She was also 'bumming' around and had taken a job at the hotel to take a break and also earn a bit of money. Roxanne was a slim beautiful girl and quite frankly when I first saw her in her waitress's gear at the hotel it was not one of those 'Wow' reactions. More like an 'Ummm – interesting', reaction. Actually. we became good friends but there was no leaping into bed as I bet you thought. Roxanne was on a different intellectual planet to me. She was into Herman Hesse and his Steppenwolf and Siddhartha novels. I had a bit of a job understanding them and they seemed a bit morbid and boring to me, but there again, maybe I didn't really understand them. But Roxanne was a free spirit and Hesse's novels were obligatory reading in those days for intellectual free spirits.

"May everyone find in it what strikes a chord in him and is of some use to him! But I would be happy if many of them were to realise that the story of the Steppenwolf pictures a disease and crisis--but not one leading to death and destruction, on the contrary: to healing."

See what I mean? Right out of my depth here. Gobbledy Gook to my simple mind.

When Roxanne changed from her waitress uniform to 'civvies' there was a total transformation. Her whole free spirit character came out and then it was 'Wow'.

So we became quite close and enjoyed each other's company and we explored together and generally had good fun.

After a few weeks work I was sufficiently solvent to hit the road again as the whole point was not to stay in one place too long just earning money. The point was to explore New Zealand and have fun. So I decided to give notice and to head off again. I asked Roxanne if she wanted to come with me and she seemed a bit noncommittal. I told her that I would be leaving on Sunday morning.

Sure enough as I walked out of the hotel that Sunday morning and hoisted my rucksack onto my back and started off down the road, there was Roxanne walking towards me with her own rucksack and ready to go. Damn but she looked good with a skimpy pair of denim shorts and her long slim tanned legs.

Okay hit the road. We hitched up to Queenstown which was easy enough and we were then going to cut across to the West Coast but we got stuck. The traffic up from Te Anau to Queenstown had made hitching a lift easy but the road out of Queenstown to the west was almost deserted. We waited and waited. A car came by and waved to us. We smiled and waved back. Stuck. More cars. Nothing. The clouds were getting lower and there was an ominous grey look to them. Sure enough the rain started. Wet, miserable and stuck.

Then a car came from the other direction and stopped opposite us. It was the same car that had gone by about three hours earlier. The one that the driver had waved to us. He leaned out and asked how we were doing. We explained that we were stuck and that there was not much traffic.

He said that it was getting late and that we should go with him back into Queenstown and stay at his house with him and his wife as we were never going to get a lift at this time in the evening. We never batted an eyelid – 'Yes thank you'.

What a marvellous experience. His wife cooked us a lovely meal and allowed us to take a bath and change into dry clothes. Then we sat around and chatted and laughed. It was the most wonderful example of genuine, no strings attached, kindness and hospitality. We were to experience this a few more times in New Zealand and it is something I will never forget.

Okay – now it was time to get some shut eye and this couple offered us a mattress that they had up on a kind of mezzanine floor. Roxanne and I cuddled down together and never left each others side for the next four months or so. Another of those wonderful relaxed, at peace relationships with no inhibitions. Love? – maybe. Hindsight would tell me 'No' but it felt like it at the time.

The next day we were up early. Profuse thanks to our hosts and off we go again with little self satisfied smiles on our faces.

We got a lift almost immediately and headed west into the mountains. Actually, we didn't go very far that day as we came across this beautiful lake and as we were in no hurry and life seemed so idyllic that we decided to ask to be dropped off there. This lake was in the middle of nowhere. There was no town or village, just this beautiful lake with some people canoeing down by the edge. Not a building in sight. It was a lovely sunny day so we climbed down to the edge of the lake and sat watching the canoeists. Life was perfect.

I think that you get the picture.

The canoeists came up and chatted to us and I asked if I could have a short paddle. This is about eight years since I had been in a canoe so I was not sure if I would remember all the little tricks. Hey, but I had to do it didn't I? I had Roxanne to impress.

So I performed a couple of quick rolls ( Eskimo rolls in the canoe that is), a couple of telemark turns and everyone clapped – bravo Trev lad – what a hero.

It really was so peaceful and calm and beautiful that we stayed there. The canoeists left and we were left on our own with not another soul in sight. Evening was coming on so we searched around a bit and found a nice spot in a clearing in the trees close to a small stream and we unrolled our sleeping bags and cuddled up again under the stars. Wonderful.

We went on like this for quite some time making our way slowly up the West Coast of the South Island then across to Wellington. Neither of us had been up towards Gisborne so we set off up the East Coast of the North Island at our usual leisurely pace. I think we both realised that I would have to fly back to Australia soon and we were just spinning it out for as long as we could.

We had arrived somewhere close to Napier early one evening and there was this lovely stretch of deserted beach. The weather was warm and fine so we decided to sleep on the beach that night. We dumped our stuff by a sand dune and went for a swim. It was still daylight but there was not a soul in sight and we had the world to ourselves – or so we thought. We were actually stark naked in an amorous embrace, compromising position, or call it what you will, when we heard this noise. It was a strange powerful noise that got louder and louder.

'What the bloody hell is that?' – Whoooosh.

Over our heads at no more than about 100 feet comes a bloody airliner. You could actually see the faces at the windows. I won't even bother to guess what they could see.

We had made our camp just over a sand dune from the end of the runway at the local airport.

'Ladies and Gentlemen, this is your captain speaking. If you look out to your left, you will see the beautiful bay of ---- -and ---er ---whooops'.

Oh well – I hope that it brightened up their evening.

Next day on to Gisborne where we had another of those wonderfully refreshing experiences of unselfish kindness. We got into the outskirts of Gisborne fairly early and decided to have a beer or two at a bar that looked quite nice. Roxanne in her little shorts did cause a head or two to turn and the next minute we were everyone's friend.

Beers were bought for us as they listened to our stories. It was good fun. There was a super older guy there that was telling the funniest jokes and generally enjoying himself. As the evening crept on we tried to make our excuses to leave so that we could find somewhere to sleep but this old fellow would have none of it. He insisted we stay at his house and we gratefully accepted. The next morning he comes into our room with tea and biscuits, explains that he has to go to work and that when we leave to just lock the door and leave the key under the mat.

Wonderful. He didn't know us from Adam.

Then it was on to Auckland to catch my plane back to Brisbane.

I had one of those cheap tickets with a fixed return date so I was stuck. I had no choice. I was also down to my last dollar. This was not very good planning but it did not worry me too much at the time. We stayed the last night with some friends from Te Anau and then early next morning I bid my farewells and headed for the airport. Quite sad to go but it had all been a wonderful experience and we promised that either I would come back to New Zealand or that Roxanne would come over to Australia. Of course it never happened. It had been fun but the love was not there.

# BACK TO AUSTRALIA

This time I was really in serious trouble when I landed back in Brisbane. As I said, I had one single Aussie dollar to my name. You might have got the impression from the tales of my youth that I am some spoilt little brat that can just call 'daddy' and he would help me out. Well, it was not like that. I was well and truly on my own. I had no reserves to call on and the lump sum total of my worldly wealth was the clothes I was standing in and the single dollar in my pocket. Luckily, I landed back in Brisbane at about midday so I had about six to eight hours to try to resolve this liquidity issue. Plenty of time. I took a deep breath and looked at my options and decided.

You know that in that kind of situation you really have to sit down, take stock and decide exactly what are your priorities. What do you need right now and what can wait?

So – I needed some food, Yep

I needed some money – Not much – but yep.

I would like to have a roof over my head for the night but that was not essential.

Everything else could wait – and exactly what more do you need than that?

Only one job that I know of that can cover the first two requirements was to go back to catering. A hotel or restaurant would do the trick. Sure enough by six o'clock that evening I had secured a job as a waiter in a good restaurant in downtown Brisbane. I still had the black trousers and white shirt from my stint in Te Anau so no further investments were needed, thankfully.

By the end of that first evening I had about fifteen dollars in tips in my pocket. I had been fed and watered and, by charming some of the other youngsters working at this restaurant, I had a floor to doss down on and a roof over my head for the night.

I was away again.

I could go on and on with these tales of where I went next, what I did next but this would just turn into one of those awful 'travelogue' type of books. Just a series of extracts from diaries. I am sure you know the kind of autobiographies I am talking about.

'That evening I had fish and chips with my friends – they were good fish and chips' Aaaaah! Horrors.

So I am going to try to stick to the main points and I am purposely going to miss out some detail as, if it did not affect my life or my way of thinking directly, then why put it in.

So here goes for a short cut:

I worked in that restaurant for a while until I had built up a small security blanket of cash then headed for the Barrier Reef and the islands again. Just for fun.

My sister was getting married in England, so I returned to Brisbane, used the return portion of my old ticket and headed back to North Yorkshire.

Easy as that – wow
    Bye Bye Aussie and New Zealand – It has been great.

Actually,
    I am missing one tiny little snippet here. I was not going to include it in my story but it happened, so why not.
    During this last little working stint in Brisbane I obviously went to a few parties as I was mixing with the young crowd at the restaurant and we also used to have a few parties at the house where I was dossing down.

At one of the parties I bumped into the lass that I had met when I first came back from that long period of sexual isolation with the seismic crew. You know – that bit about the Guinness Book of Records. Her eyes lit up when she saw me again. I had obviously impressed her. Hell, I had impressed myself. She did not waste any time and arranged to 'take me on holiday'. All expenses paid. Which she did. I am not very proud of this as I really was not interested and I still had that warm and fuzzy feeling about Roxane. I am afraid I must have been a deep disappointment to this lass and I am sorry as she was a nice person. Anyway, there's the truth of it. I became a Gigolo and not a very successful one.

# BACK IN THE UK

I had spoken to my parents on the phone occasionally from Australia. Not a lot obviously, as that is a really silly way to throw away money when you are down close to rock bottom. There were these subtle hints coming through.

'Your sister Jane's getting married you know'.

'Wouldn't it be nice to have the whole family together for her wedding?'

Little hints like that.

I think that it was time to move on anyway. I had experienced some wonderful things in my travels around Aussie and New Zealand but I needed another change. So I packed up and headed home, not telling my parents.

When I arrived at their house in North Yorkshire I just sang 'Waltzing Matilda' through the letterbox until someone came to see who was making such a terrible racket. I think that they were pleased.

After Jane's wedding (to the wrong man) I was back to square one. What to do now?

For some reason UK society doesn't seem to offer many opportunities unless you conform. My only professional qualifications were in Hotel Management and Catering and 'that is what you will bloody well do Renwick'. 'Stop trying to break out of the mould'. 'You have been trained in this and therefore that is the part you will play in your sad little existence in our society'. 'Now conform damn you'.

This was not the exciting new life with new opportunities that I had been hoping for.

Nobody was impressed with the fact that I could break-in horses or muster cattle or survive on a hamburger and a glass of milk per day. Even my excellence in Latin was not going to get me out of this vicious circle.

I got a job working in a local hotel just to make ends meet but it was horrible. Back to square one with a vengeance.

I was horrified to think that my whole life was now going to be limited to hotels and restaurants. Time to get out of this loop, at all costs.

Okay Trev – sit down and plan this out. Opportunities only come along when you go out there and look for them or you put yourself in a situation where the opportunity finds you. This was not going to happen working in the hotel business around Middlesbrough.

I was also bored with life as I perceived it in the UK. It seemed far too controlled and predictable for me.

I decided to find a job – any job – the first job I could find – but it had to be abroad.

Which I did. I answered an advertisement for cabin crew from Gulf Air out in Bahrain.

I was going to be an airline steward. Hey – it was out of the UK. It was new and I was going to make something out of this come hell or high water.

# Bahrain

I was flown out to Bahrain by Gulf Air and put up in a nice hotel on this little desert island in the Persian Gulf. It was interesting and I learnt to like and respect the Bahraini's and the other Gulf Arabs. They have a certain sophistication that you don't always see in other Arab countries, as I was to learn later on.

The other thing I liked about this new job was the training. You probably think that the training to be a steward on an aircraft is only how to serve meals from a trolley or how to pour a cup of coffee for someone without spilling it all over them. Not a bit of it. The first six months you hardly fly at all. It is heavy training on safety, how to evacuate 300 passengers from an aircraft in 30 seconds, how to find your way through parts of the aircraft in thick smoke. What to do if you have to ditch in the sea. What will happen and what to do if a plane decompresses at 35,000 feet (As a passenger they never really tell you what happens – and I am not surprised). Really quite good technical training and quite exciting too.

You are also taught how to treat major accident trauma and even taught what to do if a passenger goes into labour on a flight and how to help with the birth. They don't pull the punches on this kind of stuff either.

So it was interesting and exciting. In fact at the end of this six month training they offered me a job as an instructor in their training centre but I had other things planned by then.

What was also 'nice' about Bahrain was that there were 700 single girls on that little island and since most of the male cabin crew were a bob short of a ten shilling note (if you see what I mean) this was a very big market for a young lad. Although, maybe not so young by this stage. I must have been about 28 years old by then.

I had met Mia very early on after my arrival on Bahrain.

She was one of those tall, leggy Swedish blonds. Real Jean Shrimpton model types. In hindsight we were really not suited but we were destined to get married and spend the next seven years together. I am not going to go into this in any detail as it would be unfair to Mia. Basically we were not suited.

I was going to be magnanimous here and go on about how a breakdown of a marriage can be attributed to faults by both partners, etc., etc..

Then I thought –'Hells bells Trevor you don't really believe that, so why say it?'

Yes, I will freely admit that it was partly my fault that the marriage broke down.

The mistake I made was in marrying her in the first place!

Have you ever seen the Bill Cosby comedy programmes on the television? There is one programme where he is going to open a coffee shop and he goes to a supplier to buy one of those big coffee making machines. In front of the store are all the new modern machines but he sees an old one at the back of the store with copper tanks, brass pressure gauges and brass taps.

As he touches it there is a loud rendition of the Halleluiah chorus.

"Halleluiah, halleluiah, halleluiah".

Cosby turns to the camera and says,

"Do you know that women can't hear that"

So, of course he buys the thing and it gives him nothing but problems.

I did the same many years later with a Porsche 928. I know a bit about cars and anyone could see that this car must have been in quite a bad smash at some stage in its life. The bloody thing was bent. But all I could hear was,

"Halleluiah, halleluiah, halleluiah".

I was blinded. I did not want to see that the chassis was bent and I bought it.

Well, what a bloody expensive disaster.

Non performer with very high maintenance costs.

My marriage to Mia was the same.

I should have seen the bright red warning signs when she asked to have a bigger diamond in her engagement ring every year as a present. We were not even married when that one came out, but oh no – I had heard the chorus!

"Halleluiah, halleluiah, halleluiah".

It is funny that everyone will offer you advice and guidance, often unsolicited, when you want to buy a car,

'Don't buy that one Trevor. Very bad reputation for reliability'.

'Looks good but very poor performance'

'Very high running costs' etc., etc..

But when you are getting married nobody seems to want to step forward and throw cold water on your flames of desire. Nobody comes forward to point out that your potential partner has a screw loose or that she is only interested in money, and so on.

Why is it that our friends who would normally be more than happy to offer advice and guidance suddenly shut up and just meekly offer congratulations and best wishes when they should really be shouting out,

'Stop, don't do it!'

So I married someone totally unsuitable. Poor performer and very high maintenance costs!

Shame – but we did have some laughs and fun in the first few years.

I still have a passport with my photo inside which was the result of one of our laughs.

I had never 'done' or tried drugs. It was not really my scene. Towards the end of this six month training we became eligible for those lovely 90% discount air crew tickets. What a perk. You can fly all over the world for a few quid. The only hassle being that you have to go on standby for all the flights. But in those days this was not too much of a problem as the flights were rarely chocker block as they are nowadays.

Anyway – on with the story. This pilot friend of ours had heard that we were going to Bali and we had invited him over to our apartment for dinner so that he could tell us where to go and what to see.

He asked, 'Do you smoke?' which seemed a pretty stupid question to me as I was just lighting up another Camel.

Not that kind of smoking you dumb cluck. Oh – that marijuana stuff. Now I understood.

I told him that I had never tried it and he convinced us to give it a try.

He rolled a 'joint' there and then and after dinner we lit up. Mia had half this 'joint' and I had the other half. This did not seem much but believe me it was enough.

Literally, as we finished this joint and put it out there was a ring at the doorbell. I went out to answer it and found another friend of ours at the door.

'Come in'

This friend on the doorstep was not the kind of person that you just say,

'You'll have to excuse us but we have just smoked a joint'

So we sat there chatting as the effects of this joint took hold. We started to laugh, and we did not stop. The poor chap who had just arrived could not figure out what we were laughing at and took offence. We had to explain. By this time we were rolling around on the floor with laughter, totally out of control. This was really very rude but we really did not have any control and that is quite scary, or it was for me.

113

After everyone had gone we continued to laugh for hours on end. I did not sleep that night. I would doze off and then start chuckling and then remember some little detail of the evening and that would set me off again.

The next morning we were still chuckling and I had to go downtown to have my photo taken for a new passport. I think I was still as 'high' as a kite and I hadn't slept a wink.

As I sat down in front of the Pakistani photographer he said (have to do this with a Pakistani accent)

'No, no, no sir – eyes open please'.

That photo was in my new ten year passport and I had to live with it. Whooops.

I think that I only did about four or five flights with Gulf Air. These were mainly what we called 'round the houses' which were the little short hops around the Gulf area. It was interesting to fly down to Oman and up into Iran in those noisy little BA111's. We used to play tricks with some of the stewardesses like putting pepper in the face masks so that when they were doing the pre take off demonstrations on what to do in the event of a loss of pressure, etc., they would get a nose full of pepper and go off with streaming eyes, coughing and sneezing to the galley. Good fun.

Shortly after I arrived in Bahrain I got to know a group of guys who were working on the oil rigs in the Gulf. These lads were all quite clever and obviously enjoyed what they were doing and earning good money into the bargain. They were fit, healthy, wealthy and having a lot of fun.

They had some rather fancy apartments and houses in town and they were obviously not short of a bob or two. One house in particular was done up inside like an Arabian tent. Wonderful stereo systems, wonderful parties and quite wild.

With 700 single girls on the island all they needed was the

right contact and there would be a constant stream of beautiful Gulf Air stewardesses to brighten up their time on shore. I was that contact. Contact – not pimp by the way. The parties were wonderful. This crowd were fun and adventurous and anything was possible. We used to hire a big Dhow boat every Friday and sail out to the sand bars off the coast and take out barbeques with fillet steak, cases of wine and champagne and have a right old time. This was the life!

So in exchange for me introducing them to the girls and making sure that their parties were well attended I wanted some information from them on how to get a job in the oil industry. They were great about it. 'Try this company, try that company'. 'Their offices are here, their offices are there'. 'Go and speak to Mr. so-and-so'.

So I went round, knocking on doors (always go in person – phone calls do not work) introducing myself and trying hard to get into this new and exciting life. I think you can imagine that this was a bit of an uphill struggle. That bloody 'mould' thing again. When you are working as an airline steward you are not exactly on top of the list of candidates to work in the rough and tumble life of the oil industry. But persevere Trev lad. Which is what I did.

One day one of these lads told me to give Halliburton a go.

'Hally who'? ' Never heard of them'. I knew BP, Shell, etc., but who in heaven's name was Halliburton.

So I found out where their offices were and went along.

I was introduced to their regional maintenance manager and I proudly explained that I could change the wheel bearings on a Land Rover and that I had once rebuilt the engine on a Ferguson Tractor and could I have a job as a mechanic

How naïve, but it was worth a try.

Actually, this chap was very polite and pleasant and as I still had my upper crust British accent and obviously had spent some time at a good school he asked me more about my background. I told him about my lump sum total of 'O' levels (I didn't say how many efforts it took to acquire them!) and my limited 'A' levels in chemistry and biology.

Not really impressive stuff but he suggested that a job working in the laboratory might be more in my line than being a mechanic. He rang up the manager of the Halliburton Middle East Technical Centre and arranged for me to go downstairs to meet him. Right there and then. No appointments. No 'send your CV in, and we will let you know' type of thing. So I went downstairs and met Jeremy Rittener who was one of those wonderful, polite, quiet, cultured Englishmen who recognise talent when they see it.

We chatted about where I came from, what I had done, what my meagre qualifications were but I think Jeremy took a bit of a shine to me in a fatherly way. I think my mastery of Latin must have impressed him as there was precious little else to impress anyone.

I got the job!

Jeremy's offer was one I would use on my own step son much later on.

'We will put you on trial for a three month period. If you don't like it you can walk away, and if we don't like you, we will fire you. Okay'?

Seemed fair enough to me. I was to join Halliburton at the end of my contract with Gulf Air and I would join them on local payroll. Paid as a local Bahraini laboratory hand, no car, no housing and no expenses. I would get the grand total of the Bahrain equivalent of £300 per month.

I jumped at it and Jeremy was great. He would allow me to use his office in the evenings to watch training videos on what an oil well was, how it was drilled and all the exciting new and interesting stuff that I loved. So after all the funny odd jobs I had done in the past, here I was doing something interesting and exciting and I loved it. I spent one year in the labs at Bahrain and was then offered an international contract in Operations. This was going somewhere. These guys in Operations were the heroes. These guys were the clever buggers that kept the money rolling into the Halliburton coffers which unfortunately would be forgotten in the years to come as we became managed more and more by lawyers and accountants. Never mind, at that stage Halliburton still had its feet firmly on the ground and was not obsessed with the latest managerial jargon and the teachings of the latest managerial guru. God – there were sad days to come but back then we were still managed by guys who had come up through the ranks and knew what was needed, how and when. These were the glorious days and I was to be part of it.

It was during my stay in Bahrain that the Queen, you know, Lizzy II, ERII, who I had run off the road back in my Balmoral days, came to visit the Emir. I was not sure what these two were going to have in common as the Emir, Sheik Iza Bin Sulman Al Khalifir, known affectionaly in expat circles as Shakey Baby, was a bit of a character. He did have a very famous horse breeding centre on the island and I am sure that this would give them some common ground. The Emir was a short rather round man and he was an absolute pleasure to know. He had a large family of brothers but I never met his wife and sisters and they were never mentioned. He ran Bahrain through his family of brothers and sons, as do most Arab countries in the Gulf. Democracy doesn't really suit most Gulf States and they run very efficiently under a sort of wise, benevolent, capitalist, dictatorship. Hey – Don't knock it. It works and works very well.

The Emir had a lovely beach house, which overlooked a pristine private area of the west shore. No Bahraini was allowed anywhere near the place but all the expats and especially the expat girls had an open invitation to go there every weekend to sunbathe and swim. So there was quite a bit of young 'talent' on the beach to brighten up the day. The evenings were spent partying in his beach house.

There was a hostess at these parties to make sure everyone was in the right mood and enjoying themselves. It was truly, let your hair down, and anything else you wanted to let down, type of parties. In fact this hostess, who was Swiss, I think, used to get everyone into the swing of it by singing 'Everybody get them off' and then promptly throw her knickers, or pretend to throw her knickers, into the chandeliers. Kind of wild, as I am sure you have gathered by now. Actually, I only ever went to one of these parties, something to do with wrong sex and lack of tits. I am sure that if I had been equipped with the latter, the former might not have been a significant factor. Life was a bit like that there.

Anyway, here comes ER II and I could not see her dancing around the chandelier, singing 'everybody get them off'. The Emir must have had the same thoughts as he organised some camel races and tours of his Arabian horse stud farm. Nothing there to upset the Royal equilibrium.

So off I went with a few hundred other expats to see Her Majesty at the camel races. It was all nicely informal and she passed through the onlookers, nodding her greetings.

That is when I realised that I had not gone there to see her. I had gone there for her to see me! I was waiting for her to catch my eye and waiting for that sparkle of recognition, but of course it never happened.

What in heaven's name did you expect Trevor?

'Trev lad, how great to see you again'. Big hug.

'You must come round and see us at the palace'.

'How's the rabbit shooting going?'

'Wonderful to see you again'. 'Bye'.

Hey Ho – Stupid boy.

We had some really wonderful characters working and living in Bahrain. Some of these expats had been there for ten years or more. There was one lovely girl there and it always brings a smile to my face when I remember her. She was terribly, terribly upper crust and spoke with a slow, relaxed, aristocratic drawl. She did not give a damn what anyone thought of her and she would have the most amazing parties and the gin and tonic would flow like water. Rumour had it that she got through a bottle of gin a day and it would not surprise me.

She always made an effort to communicate with the plebeian scum. You know, mixing in with the peasants and we 'peasants' would be invited to her parties, some of which started at midday and went on to the early hours of the next day. The food she put on was always something special. It was not lobster, fillet or anything like that. She always made an effort to be sure we 'peasants' were comfortable. No nasty surprises on the plate. Something we were used to (in her mind). So she would serve up Bangers, Mash & Mushy Peas, Toad in the Hole, etc., etc.. Those parties were hilarious and she was a wonderful character, as you have probably gathered by now.

This same lass also used to swear like a trooper, but always in the nicest possible accent of course. Once day as she was driving back from the airport the boot lid of the old car she was driving literally fell off into the middle of the road. She stopped to pick it up and a passing policeman stopped to help her. He asked if it was a hired car. Her response was,

"Do you think for one minute I would rent a fucking wreck like this". Lovely.

Another time the Chief Stewardess at Gulf Air called her into the office and suggested that she should try changing her hair style.

"Why not try plaits"

Another classic response.

"If my mother wanted me to wear my hair in fucking plaits she would have called me Heidi"

Wonderful.

Let's get back to Halliburton. I am not going to go into all the technical details of what we did in 'Operations' but it was all exciting stuff. I was on one of the 'Stimulation boats' which were rather large supply boats converted to pumping all kinds of stuff into oil wells. We used to sail up and down the Gulf, stopping off in Dubai and back into Bahrain to reload various chemicals, acids and other material needed for the jobs. We were so busy in those days that I was actually 'offshore' for most of each month and only managed to grab a day or two at a time, while in Bahrain, to take a break. I was on a 'Live-In' contract by this stage and Halliburton provided married quarters for Mia and me, but as she was still flying with Gulf Air and I was offshore most of the time, we rarely saw each other. I also had to attend various training courses in the USA so that also added to my time away from home.

I have to mention the quality of management we had in Halliburton in those days as those guys were really quite exceptional. They had been there, done it and got the Tee shirt and knew what was needed, how and when.

Mia and I had been trying to have a baby and she was having some difficulty keeping pregnancies going. In fact she had two or three miscarriages and it was not pleasant for her.

One day I was down in the southern part of the Gulf anchored off an island just to the east of Qatar, waiting to tie up to a rig nearby to 'stimulate' the well they had just drilled. I got a radio call from Larry who was our big boss up in Bahrain. I mean not just immediate boss. He was the 'Big Boss' of all Halliburton Operations in the Southern Gulf region, from Kuwait to India. So – Big Cheese. That's what I am trying to say.

'Trevor – if we send a helicopter over the back of the boat could it pick you up from there?'

'Yes, Larry, but we are close to Halul island and it has a jetty so we could easily pull anchors and go alongside', I said. 'What's this about?'

'Oh nothing really we just have a very important job to do up in Kuwait and we want you on it', Larry replied. 'So if we send a chopper out from Doha it could pick you up and take you back to Doha where we would have the Halliburton aircraft standing by to bring you in. Does that sound okay?'

'Yes that's fine, Larry. Just let us know when we need to move'. I replied.

Not more than 30 minutes after this radio call, the rig called to say that they would not need our services after all so we were free to pull anchors and head back to base. So I radio'd back to Bahrain and got hold of Larry to let him know we were on our way back and should be alongside the jetty in Bahrain at about three in the morning.

'That's great Trevor. See you there'.

And he was. At three in the morning there were Larry and the Marine Services Manager waiting on the jetty as we tied up.

'Trevor, nothing to worry about but Mia is in the International Hospital and she may be miscarrying but she is fine'.

This was a major effort by Larry and his team to go out of their way and do whatever was needed to get me back to Bahrain as quickly as possible. It was something I was never to forget and was a wonderful example of good and caring management. This incident secured my loyalty for many a long year.

There were many examples of this thoughtfulness and effort. I wish we saw it nowadays but sadly it has been lost to the faceless style of modern management.

Another wonderful example was a much sadder affair where we lost twelve operations staff in a single year. It's worth pointing out that we were a fairly small group of people working in the Gulf in those days and we all knew each other.

It was in 1978. The first accident was onshore up in Iran where a team had set up their equipment next to a well head in the evening and were waiting for first light to start a pumping operation. What they didn't know, and nobody knew, was that this well was in poor condition and was actually leaking gas which was permeating up through the ground.

There was no wind and this well was in the bottom of a whaddi or gully. The gas built up during the night and exploded at first light when the team went to switch off the arch lights. There were five guys killed that day and it took them a long time to die. As usual in these countries the wheels of bureaucracy turn awfully slowly. If I remember correctly is took about two days to get the surviving burns victims on a special air ambulance out of the country but neither made it.

There were another couple of individual accidents that year and then the last one that effected me badly as it involved the boat and the crew that I worked with.

I had been working on the boat, the Midnight Moon, for about two years by this stage and we were a very close team. The boat had been down to Dubai to load up some equipment for a special job up by Kuwait. We then set sail for Bahrain where the materials that were going to be needed were to be loaded. When we got to Bahrain, I got off the boat as Mia was having some minor medical problems and it was decided that I should stay on shore to look after her. Two days later the boat capsized and five of the crew were killed and of the eleven others on board many were lucky to be rescued. No 'Mayday' signal was sent out and the first anyone knew about it was two days later when a passing freighter saw survivors in the water.

It was another of those bloody chain of events catastrophes that should have been easy to stop but nobody 'broke the chain' and the tragic outcome became unavoidable.

I won't go into all the details as it is not part of this book and it would not be fair to the people involved. After all, they were there and I was not. That's their story, not mine. Apparently, there were some very impressive acts of bravery, perseverance and determination. Suffice it to say that it effected me very deeply as you can probably gather.

The last survivors were rescued five days after the boat went down which is a long time to be floating around the Gulf in a life ring or Norwegian Float with no water, no food and the fish nibbling at you.

Two of the five that died in that accident could not be accounted for and it was a fair assumption that they had gone down with the boat. One was Johnny who was my immediate supervisor and he and I had shared a cabin for the last two years so we were pretty close. Johnny was well respected within Halliburton and it was decided to make the maximum effort to try to recover his body from the wreck. This was not just to reach closure but also to help his poor wife out as there is some stupid insurance rule that if the body is not recovered the widow has to wait two years for the insurance company to pay out.

So Halliburton kitted out another of the Stimulation Boats with compressors, diving gear, decompression chambers and a team of professional divers and they asked me to go up with the divers to the wreck site as I knew the boat and the layout of the equipment and cabins and might be able to help.

Do you know, it took us two days to find the position where the boat had gone down. You would think that it would be easy to find the wreck. After all we had a pretty good idea where it had gone down and there were about six other vessels in the area trying to find it. We went back and forth in a search grid pattern for two whole days trying to find it. I spent most of my time way up in the crows nest as you could see for miles from there and also I think I needed the solitude. We were getting desperate and had the depth sounder on, hoping that it would show on that. A few times we stopped over a likely target and quickly sent the divers down to check it out. Nothing. Back and forth we went. Nothing.

Eventually when we found the wreck we were amazed why we had taken so long to locate it. There were the mooring ropes floating up from the sea bed and a small slick from the leaking fuel tanks. It was really quite visible but it gives you some idea how difficult it is to find a sunken boat out at sea. The proverbial needle in a haystack.

We laid anchors over the wreck site and the divers got ready for their gruesome task. By this time the boat had been down for about ten days and at a depth of about 150 feet (the divers amongst you will understand the relevance of this) and we all knew that the next few hours were not going to be pleasant.

Johnny could not swim and I guessed that we would find his body inside the boat. The divers also had experience in this kind of thing and correctly guessed that a non swimmer would retreat to the inside of the boat as it went down, rather than face the panic of jumping into the sea knowing that you cannot swim. Strange how the human mind can make you do the most irrational things.

Sure enough we found his body in the cabin that he and I used to share. I won't go into the details of getting his body out and back onto the search vessel. I was able to identify him (just) and radioed back to Bahrain that we had found him. Sad.

No other bodies were found, so we pulled anchors and headed home.

I continued to work in the Gulf for about another year after that and we did some interesting stuff. One that sticks in my mind was going up to Iran waters where they had a huge blow out on one of their offshore rigs. They had hit a huge high pressure gas pocket and they had lost control of the well. We were sent up to just pump water over the abandoned rig to stop it catching fire until Red Adair and his merry boys could get to it. We came up to it in the middle of the night in the pitch dark. No moon and no lights from the rig. It was ghostly. But it was the noise that was amazing. We could hear the roar of this beast from over ten kilometres away. As we got closer it was a really deafening roar. Maybe if you can imagine ten Concordes taking off at the same time and you are only 100 yards away might come close to it. The whole rig and surrounding area was swathed in a fine mist with the well blowing out through the middle of it. It was eerie.

If that beast had caught light there would have been one hell of an explosion. We did not anchor as it was too dangerous to be in one fixed position so we just stayed up wind of the beast and pumped like crazy for two days straight until some help arrived and was able to take over.

The next few months were quite eventful as Iran fell apart. I had been up there doing some special jobs and it was interesting to travel around the countryside. Iranians have this wonderful habit of driving at night without any lights – I figured out that they thought they were saving electricity. As we travelled down from Ahvaz to the port of Bouchir there were military everywhere and all kinds of checkpoints. Nobody could tell me what was going on and they all said this was most unusual. Sure enough about three weeks later the whole place went to

125

hell in a basket and we had to get everyone out of there in a hurry.

While we were in Bouchir we very nearly got arrested and maybe we were close to being shot as well. These army lads were so jumpy it could have gone either way. We had brought the nitrogen pumping units all the way down from Ahvaz and the liquid nitrogen had been sent across from Bahrain in their giant vacuum flasks on the back of one of our boats. I won't bore you with the technical details but you cannot fully check the pumping units without the liquid nitrogen so in reality the units we took down to Bouchir were untried and untested. Obviously, the first thing I had to do was to hook up the tanks to the units and pump a bit to check them out. Well by the time we got to the boat and had the suction lines rigged up it was about one o'clock in the morning. I didn't bother to fit any discharge lines from the pumps, so the high pressure pump outlet was just open to the atmosphere. These were big pumps and the volume of nitrogen gas that comes out of them is incredible.

So there we were at one o'clock in the morning with the area around us swathed in the heavy clouds of condensation from the cold nitrogen and then I kicked the pumps into gear. Oh dear me. It was like a whole squadron of jet fighters taking off. What a racket.

Before we could say 'Boo' – two army trucks swooped down on us and the next minute we were surrounded by some very nervous soldiers all with their rifles pointed directly at us.

It took quite a long time to reassure them that we were not some invading force but they still could not understand the swirling mist and the racket we had caused.

I must take my hat off to the local Halliburton management at the time. As soon as it became clear that Iran was falling apart and we would have to get everyone and their families out of there, they did not hesitate. They went to Gulf Air and chartered two Gulf Air Tri Stars ( you know – the big Lockheed airliners) and started running them round the clock up to Abadan in south west Iran to bring everyone out. Good old Halliburton told everyone, employees, customers, absolutely everyone that they should make their way to the airport with one bag per person and no more than one pet and get on the planes to get them back to Bahrain and safety. It was impressive. There was no hassle of bureaucracy, agreements or contracts between companies. Halliburton grabbed the bull by the horns, decided what had to be done, knew that it was an emergency and got going. Wonderful.

I don't suppose there are many employees or customers left working out there who were rescued by Halliburton in those days but believe me, the company earned many years of 'Brownie Points' for what they did then. Good for you Halliburton. The good old days.

While we are at this point I must tell you a couple of tricks we used to play on any trainees that came onto the Stimulation Boats we had in the Gulf. Most of these boats were equipped with 'Burners' which were huge flares to burn the oil or gas from the wells. These burners were mounted onto long booms that swung out from the front of the boats. The purpose of these burners was to flow back oil wells to clean them up or test their production rates, so that you could burn off the oil instead of just dumping it or transferring it to tankers. Obviously, this is quite a dramatic exercise and we always had photos of these huge flames to impress any visitors. I'm sure you have seen films of oil wells on fire at the end of the first Iraq war and apart from the fact that we used to add air to the flames to keep them 'smokeless' the intensity is about the same.

Before we opened the well we would get one of the new trainees, casually give him a box of matches and tell him to walk down the flare boom to light the flame. All these poor trainees had seen so far were these photos of the huge flames and they imagined themselves standing a couple of feet away from this potential inferno as they threw matches into it. Of course we did not tell them they were only lighting the small propane pilot light. It would have ruined all the fun.

"Get down there lad – what are you waiting for" Ha ha. Cruel really, but everyone got a laugh out of it in the end and it was not done maliciously. We had all been though these initiation pranks and it did no harm that I could see.

The other naughty we used to do before flaring was to get the group together and very seriously read through the safety procedures. These safety procedures were written by someone who had probably never been to the Gulf or been anywhere near one of these flares. There was one section of this safety manual that stated that whenever flaring operations were taking place there had to be one person standing by in a full fire suit with breathing apparatus.

"That's your job Jimmy" we would say to some luckless trainee.

"Go and get kitted up"

This poor lad would put on one of those bulky, silver fire suits, with a full hood and face shield and an air bottle strapped to his back under the suit. He had to stand up by the bridge of the boat and once he was in position we would open the well and start flaring.

You could visibly see the discomfort. Shifting from leg to leg. Turning round to look at everyone to see what was going on or if he was going to be given some new instruction. Nothing. Just stay there.

The Gulf is incredibly hot and humid and you are sweating profusely most of the time let alone in a fire suit.

Eventually the poor lad would not be able take it any more and the hood would come off, then the jacket, then the gas bottle and this poor bugger would be dripping with sweat. Not just dripping – drenched.

We would all be splitting our sides with laughter.

"Buggers!" And off he would stomp in a right old huff.

Another funny that appealed to my sense of humour.

Way back there was a big blow out just off the coast of Dubai. Halliburton was called to do the pumping and this was a very big job. Masses of pumping equipment had to be loaded onto a huge barge and then be towed out to pump into a relief well to try to kill this beast.

(A 'relief' well is when you drill another well adjacent to the one blowing out so that you can intersect with the well bore of the blow out and pump into it several thousand feet underground. That way you can pump into it at the source of the problem).

The well was blowing out from the sea bed and was coming up as gas but it had not ignited so the sea was just bubbling, in a rather nasty, ominous, threatening way. One stupid supply boat captain actually sailed right through this at one stage and how he never sank or ignited the thing we will never know. He did it on purpose as well – the fool. Someone should have reminded him of Archimedes Principle.

Anyway, once we got pumping it was a non stop operation to try to kill this well. The pumping went on for day after day at full rate. At one stage the supervisor on the job got his tank measuring stick – a really big one – hung it overboard into the sea, pulled it out, looked very carefully at the level mark and declared,

"Keep pumping lads, we still have a long way to go by the looks of it".

Loved it.

Was that too technical? I hope not.

One of my endearing memories of my time on these boats in the Gulf was pulling anchors and sailing away from a rig or platform after a job. A lot of these jobs took quite a time to complete and we were sometimes up for 24 to 36 hours without a break. At the end of the job we would rig down the treatment lines and gather up all our equipment and secure it back on the boat. Then we would caste off the lines and pull anchors and then sail away. It was a wonderful feeling to be physically tired and sit there on the back deck and watch the rig slowly disappear into the distance in the normally still waters of the Gulf.

I spent many hours up on the prow of the boat as we sailed up and down the Gulf. Dolphins would play in front of us for hours on end and I could happily watch them as they effortlessly ducked and weaved in front of our bow wave. Another thing that sticks in my mind was watching the flying fish. I had never seen these before and to see them gliding over the surface of the water was fascinating. They could 'fly' or glide for a hell of a long way and occasionally they would just drop their tail into the water and just give it a couple of quick flicks to get airborne again. That was beautiful to watch.

# EGYPT

In about late 1979 we had transferred an old, run down, mangy, Nitrogen Pumping unit from our operations in the Gulf to Egypt. Egypt wanted one, they were willing to pay for it, so what do we do? We find the oldest, most run down piece of junk we have and ship it off to Halliburton in Egypt. But these things come back to haunt you.

'Trevor – we would like you to go to Egypt to set up Nitrogen Operations there, get the operations going and train the new operators'. Ha ha

Yes it happened. That will teach you to transfer junk Renwick.

So I transferred to Egypt and spend the first four months or so down in Ras Shu Kheir which is on the west side of the Gulf of Suez, just about 20 kilometres south of where Moses parted the seas and took the Israelites across to safety. Seriously, there is a signpost marking the spot. I wonder how they knew.

So there I was with this run down heap of junk trying to get it to function correctly. I had not paid any attention to the required supply of liquid nitrogen as we had a letter from the Egyptian gas company saying that they could supply 20,000 litres per day which was more than enough for what we needed. So I fiddled with the pumping unit until the day came where I was happy that everything was working right. Time to go and get some of that liquid nitrogen and put this beast through its paces. Up to Cairo I went and a driver took me to the local gas plant. I met the manager and he proudly took me to see his liquid nitrogen storage tanks and the area where we could load up. As I came round the corner, there ahead of me was this small tank, about twice the size of an oil drum. Shame

– the manager was smiling proudly and pointing to his storage tank.

I think we must have had a language barrier. 'Yes, he could produce 20 litres per day – wasn't that wonderful'. One of those decimal point problems. I think even NASA has them from time to time.

What to do ? This wasn't enough to even prime up our pumps. Oh dear me. Back to the Halliburton office and explain the problem to the big boss.

Now the fun began. You would be surprised how many places actually manufacture liquid nitrogen (I am sure that you are really interested in this, aren't you?) so I convinced the boss to let me loose with a driver and go all over Egypt to find a suitable source.

Hey – this was okay!

I went everywhere, north, south east and west. I visited their air force. They had the nitrogen but wouldn't let me have any, not surprisingly. I visited a fertiliser plant up in Alexandria. Yes, they had it and produced excess but it was all plumbed into the centre of their plant and there was no way we could get our big trucks in to load up. Eventually, I found what I was looking for in Helwan, which is just south of Cairo. So I had toured Egypt, had a good time and their Nitrogen Operations were up and running. Time to move on.

Before I do, I must tell you about a very embarrassing event that happened to me in Egypt. This is not for the sensitive readers, so you might want to skip a page or two if you think you may be offended.

While I was in Ras Shu Kheir I started to get a urinary track infection and after a couple of days my kidneys were hurting so I made arrangements to go up to Cairo to see a doctor.

I knew there was an American Hospital in Cairo and assumed that they would have some pretty good facilities to deal with my minor ailment. Wrong! Aren't these assumptions dangerous and I keep making them.

The doctor at the American Hospital (American in name only) decided that I need to have an X-Ray but of course he did not have an X-ray machine. So he made the arrangements with a specialist down town and off I went into the famous Cairo traffic. Three hours later and five kilometres away I arrived at the radiologist to be briefly examined and then given a long list of medicines and other odds and sods that I had to buy. I was not to eat that evening and I was to drink the entire contents of a large bottle of castor oil that was on the list before I went to bed. I was to come into his offices at seven o'clock the next morning with the balance of this shopping list to have the X-Rays taken.

What a bloody awful night. I had never had 'the castor oil treatment' before and I was not really prepared for the consequences. Bloody hell – I was drained, I was empty, I had not slept a wink. It was awful. The toilet – nature's great leveller.

Okay so off I went to the radiologist where a short, rather grubby assistant informed me that now I had to have an enema. Oh Noooo! Now that is a humbling experience. Then this little bugger told me that I had to have a second one – the little pervert. I think he might have been involved in the Suez war fiasco and was trying in his subtle way to punish an Englishman. I promised him that I was more than 'empty' but he insisted. Forget any British stiff upper lip or any of that rubbish, I was at the lowest point in my life. Ahh, but he had one more trick up his sleeve.

He fished around in my shopping bag of medicines and informed me that I now had to have an injection of something-or-other, which would then shrink the poor abused bowel. He had the old reusable needle and syringe boiling away in a saucepan on a gas stove and that is what he used to administer this injection. It makes you cringe nowadays doesn't it?

Injection over he sent me back to the waiting room, which now had three or four other people waiting there.

He was right about the shrinking of the bowel. My bowel was now empty, but shrink it did, and there I was sitting in this waiting room with uncontrollable farts. Totally uncontrollable, and repetitive. Bloody hell – when is this all going to finish! The humiliation was total.

And they weren't finished with this nightmare yet.

I was called in to the X-ray room and put on the table and then strapped down. The doctor explained that he was going to start injecting some barium dye into my blood stream. He then lined up about six very large brown vials. Yes, he was going to inject the whole lot – Oh Nooo!

'Nurse', he said, 'keep talking to Mr. Renwick and watch his eyes very carefully'.

'What's going on here?' I asked, 'Is this dangerous?'

'Not really', he explained, 'but some people do go into an allergic shock reaction but if that happens we have these other injections which you bought that can stop you going into a coma'.

Oh dear, dear me. Never again will I go running to the doctor. Just get some antibiotics, steal some antibiotics, eat mouldy bread, anything, but never, never, never will I go through that again.

For all you sensitive readers you can now open your eyes and read on. I promise no more lavatorial revelations.

One more story though before we move on.

The Egypt offices also acted as the regional offices for some operations we had down in Sudan. One day the boss asked me to come into the office to help out on a little problem he had. Little problem – Ha. There was one of our poor operators who had been flown back out of Sudan and was in a hell of a state in the boss's office. The guy had cracked up completely. Our jobs can be a bit hairy and stressful from time to time and normally we try to relieve that stress by drinking copious amounts of alcohol. I suspect that Kartoum was a bit short on the alcohol supply and this lad had tried some other form of stress relief. Personally, I think this guy had smoked the wrong weed or something similar. It was a hot summer day and he was dressed up in pullovers, scarves, woolly hat, gloves, heavy winter boots, jacket and every other piece of Arctic clothing that you could imagine. Actually his speech was quite coherent and if it was not for the clothes you would think that he was completely normal. However, as he chatted away to the boss he stood up out of the chair and started to take these clothes off – and he did not stop. The next minute this guy was stark naked and still continuing his conversation as if nothing was wrong. The grand finale was when he then did a head stand against the wall and still continued his conversation, stark bollock naked, upside down. Weird.

Once we got him back into his clothes there was no doubt that this chap was going to have to be flown home for some treatment and so I was given the job of babysitting him that evening and someone else was given the job of flying back to the US with him.

I got him back to our staff house and he was fine. Chatting away and relaxing as if nothing was wrong. So after getting him fed and watered I showed him to his room and off he went to bed.

Ahhhah – The next morning he was not there. He was not in the house, he had not gone to the offices. Oh hell's bells. The bugger's escaped!

The police eventually found him walking through downtown Cairo in his underwear.

I had done my bit, not very successfully, so I handed him over to the care of the other poor chap that had to fly all the way back to the States with him. Not funny.

During this time Mia had moved back to Sweden to try to carry her third pregnancy through safely. I was commuting back and forth from Cairo to Stockholm and generally doing my impressions of a high flying oil field executive (as they call them nowadays on the news). In reality, just an 'operator', but a good one, mark you. Mia was still having problems with her pregnancy and we spent a lot of the time at the Karlinska hospital doing tests, tests and more tests. Eventually, with about three weeks to go to her term they suggested that she be admitted so that she could be under closer observation. Actually, it was a very good thing that I did attend all those tests with her as by now I had a fair idea of what instrument showed what and what it should be reading. The day came when they called me to say that they were now going to induce and that I should get to the hospital as soon as possible. As Mia lay there they attached all the monitors probes and bells and whistles and even inserted a small probe into the skull of the baby. Amazing.

They confirmed that everything was looking good so they would wait a while before going into the delivery room. At that point they all left the room. There was Mia lying back there with wires and suction pads all over. I was holding her hand and watching the monitors. Baby's heart rate – 130, good, 120 okay, 100 what's going on, 90 hey hold on, 80 oh bloody hell – Press the alarm button and in they came a-running. They took one look at the monitors and started to sprint down the corridor to the operating theatre pushing Mia ahead of them on the hospital gurney. The Gynaecologist was relaxed and just turned to me.

'I'm afraid you will have to stay here Trevor. Just wait over there in the waiting room and I will get back to you as soon as I can'. And off he jogged to the operating theatre.

It was an emergency caesarean and thank God we were right there in the hospital. Poor Christian came out a bit blue and after about an hour they wheeled him into where I was sitting in the waiting area and the doctor came to tell me that everything was alright but they had to rush a bit. I cried.

Where to next? I had done my work in Egypt and had been there, on and off, for about a year. I had seen the country, visited the pyramids, had my photograph taken sitting on a camel in front of the Great Pyramid. That is obligatory by the way and matches the one of my father in exactly the same spot, sitting there on his camel, looking very smart in his Royal Army Medical Corp uniform.

That was another strange feeling. To be exactly where my father had been in that far and distant land some forty years earlier. I got the same feeling going up inside the Great Pyramid at Giza. When you go inside this pyramid there is not some huge entrance door and an escalator to take you up to the centre of the pyramid. It might have changed now but when I visited it there was just a small opening in the side of the pyramid and then a very narrow steep staircase leading up inside to the burial chamber. It was so narrow that two people could barely pass each other. This long inclined narrow passage was lit by a string of bare light bulbs hanging from an electrical cable. I knew my father had gone into the pyramid when he was there and it was a strange feeling to know that I was placing my footsteps exactly where my father had placed his, way back in 1944. Also to stand in the very small burial chamber in the middle of the pyramid knowing that my father had stood in the very same spot and had probably had the same thoughts of wonder that I was experiencing. Nice feeling in a way.

I wonder how they cope now that Egypt has opened up to tourism. There is no way that you can get hundreds of people up into that pyramid let alone the thousands that now visit Giza. I don't know. Maybe it is closed to visitors or perhaps they really do have a giant entrance hall and an escalator. I hope not.

So I had 'done' Egypt and it was interesting. I had visited the Cairo museum and seen all those marvellous displays and had seen the mask and mummy of 'Toot, I'm Coming'. Time to move on.

# ALGERIA

Back in 1980 Halliburton transferred me to Algeria. Hassi Messaoud to be exact.

Over the years I was to get to know Algeria very well. In fact I was to be assigned to Algeria three times. I am still on my third assignment there as I write this tale.

I like Algeria. I like deserts and the Sahara takes some beating. I know that it must not be everyone's cup of tea, but I like it. The desert can be quite beautiful. I still find it beautiful, in a harsh unforgiving way. You know, when I was about twelve or thirteen I had this dream to drive through the Sahara in a Land Rover and now someone was paying me to fulfil one of my childhood dreams. There is another aspect about deserts that I find enthralling. I had my first experience of deserts in Australia and it was the same feeling I had then as I now had in the Sahara. As you walk about, or go camping, or just climb to the top of a sand dune or go arrow head hunting in a whaddi you have a realisation that you are probably walking where no other human being has every walked before. Sure, there must have been human's somewhere near at some point in time but not that exact spot. I have always found that quite exciting. Don't ask me why as I haven't got a clue. Just one of my little quirks.

What was a real winner on this assignment is that some country manager, in his wisdom, had decided that all expats working in Algeria would be on live in contracts, living on the Mediterranean island of Mallorca and commuting into Algeria on a two weeks on duty and one week off duty schedule. In hindsight and having been in management myself, this was downright stupid but who were we to argue. Live in Mallorca, house rents paid for, heating and electricity paid for, kids schooling paid for. Wow – may this last forever – but it didn't, of course. But it did last for four years and boy, oh boy, those four years were fun.

To tell the truth we had some supervisors in Algeria at that time that I can only describe as oxygen thieves. Not all, but there were two or three that were absolutely useless. We even called one of them 'Zero'. That was a measure of his capability.

'Zero' was a short American from Oklahoma and he was not really at home in Algeria. Nervous type, if you know what I mean.

He regularly spent his evenings playing poker with his friends of the same ilk, so we decided to play a little trick on him, which very nearly backfired. It was in 1982 and the UK was having its problems with Argentina over the Falkland Islands. We had got hold of an FM cordless microphone and arranged that one of the lads who was playing poker that night with Zero would ask for the radio to be switched on at exactly seven p.m. so that he could listen to the news, 'as he had heard that there was some rioting in Algiers'. That was the excuse. As he switched on the radio to the frequency pre-set to the microphone we were ready outside.

'This is the BBC World Service. Here is the seven o'clock news'

'Reports are coming in of violent rioting in the city of Algiers and the surrounding countryside. Rioting mobs are attacking foreign interests and several foreign workers have been killed as these riots spread throughout the country. Latest reports indicate that this rioting has spread to the oilfields around Hassi Messaoud and that foreign workers are being targeted.'

The effect was dramatic. Zero went white. He jumped up from the card table and rushed outside. The next thing we knew he had jumped into his Chevy and was driving out of the base as fast as he could go. Oh – bloody hell. We had to scramble into my Chevy and take off after him. The silly idiot was on the road to Algiers and he was going to get out of this country come hell or high water. We eventually caught up with him and tried to explain that it was all a joke. I don't think he was very amused but we didn't hear any more about it. I suppose he was too embarrassed to make the whole incident public knowledge.

After this he became a butt for our jokes and tricks. The poor chap was a bag of nerves so we used to help things along by setting off acetylene bombs outside his room. These can be quite impressive if you get it right. You get a large plastic rubbish bag and then you fill it with about ¼ acetylene gas and ¾ oxygen. You then tie the neck of the inflated bag and attach a piece of toilet paper which you set light to so that it is just smouldering. When the smouldering loo paper touches the plastic and melts it and ignites the gas mixture inside there is one hell of bang. Sometimes it's just a whoosh if the mixture is not quite right but either way it is quite impressive. Bloody dangerous as well.

Poor old Zero never knew who was doing this to him. We would be long gone by the time the bag exploded. Whooosh – 'Who did that?. I'll get you, you bastards!'

Poor lad. It wasn't long before he decided that Algeria did not suit him and he returned to the security of Oklahoma. For Good – Everyone's good!

I was now living in Mallorca and Mia and my son Christian had moved from Stockholm to join me. I had already rented a nice villa in Bon Aire which is a lovely little development to the east side of the Bay of Pollensa. I had seen this villa in the late summer and thought that it would suit us, just fine. What I did not know was that this development was purely holiday homes. Have you ever lived in a completely deserted village or town? It must be about the same. By October this little development was completed deserted. There was not a soul to be seen. Not a single house light to be seen.

I don't suppose there was another human being within three miles. It was weird. I went outside one evening and shouted at the top of my voice,

'Is anyone out there?'

All that came back were the echoes. Very strange. I don't mind living in a cave, or in a wood, or in total isolation in a desert, but to be surrounded by dark, empty houses was quite disconcerting.

In order for Mia to enjoy a more relaxed, less stressful life (touch of sarcasm Trevor you naughty boy) she made arrangements to have an Au Pair girl from Sweden for a year at a time. She planned to have a new Au Pair each Christmas. A couple of years after moving to Mallorca I came back in early January after a long stint in the desert. The new Au Pair girl had arrived from Sweden and she was not the usual Swedish beauty. In fact she was short, plump and spotty and had this ridiculous red ribbon wound in a bow on her head.

I told Mia that if that was my Christmas present – I didn't want it. Ha, ha.

My son Christian had a lovely time there. He was still an infant but the days were filled with sun and fun. By this time I had bought an old Century Resorter speed boat that had been sunk and I had bought it for a song and spent about eighteen months rebuilding it.

It was now an immaculate, mahogany power boat which we used for skiing and going out diving. Christian used to sit in my lap steering as we roared across the bay. He loved it.

He was a bright lad and spoke Swedish and English fluently and was picking up Mallorcian at his play school. He was a bit short of expat friends though and that was a shame.

142

We eventually moved house to a lovely old 'finca' (farmhouse) nearer to the village of Pollensa as being stuck in that tourist development was no fun. All the resident expats lived nearer to the main centres and our social life did not suit being stuck out in the deserted development of Bon Aire. This finca was owned by a very strange American lady. She later showed us a magazine article from the New Yorker of her 5th marriage where she and her new husband were married while on horse back and dressed in pink satin. Pink cowboy boots as well! See what I mean? She was proud of it too. She was obviously not short of a bob or two and the house was fully furnished and decorated – original Picasso's and Salvador Dali's on the walls – Bloody hell. We had to draw up some special clauses in that rental agreement to make sure that we would not be held responsible for any losses or theft.

We only stayed there about one year and then I bought a lovely old Finca on the hillside between Pollensa and Alcudia. It was really nice. Small but nice. The walls were about a metre thick and it had a very old, stone bread oven built onto the side of the house. Now that is the way to cook. If you are having an evening dinner party you fire up this old bread oven and throw wood in until it is roaring. Then you let it burn down until there are just embers. You scrape the embers to the sides and then you put a whole lamb or suckling pig in a roasting tray and stick it inside the oven. Brick up the entrance to the oven and then off you go the beach for five or six hours. Come back and it is cooked to perfection.

You may have noticed that I have hardly mentioned my parents since the time when I returned to the UK from Australia. Quite frankly, my father was still working at that point and with me being stationed in Egypt and the Middle East it was just not possible for them to visit me. It was only when we moved to Mallorca that we came back into striking range. As the years went by I was to see much more of them but I do regret that I did not spend more time with my father as his health was deteriorating. My mother always says that she wishes that he had lived longer as he would have been proud of me. That is just her way of saying that my poor father did not have a clue what I did for a living and probably thought that I was just a roustabout or roughneck on a rig.

Anyway, they came out to visit us in Mallorca a couple of times after my father retired. Unfortunately, on his second visit my father had a stroke and although he recovered to a large extent he was basically incapacitated from then on. He could still walk about unaided but he was not allowed to drive a car and that upset him more than anything else.

Unfortunately I had to go back to work and I had to leave Mia to deal with this awful situation. Mia was superb. She was really quite efficient and dealt with the situation very well and spent most days running Mum up and down the island to and from the hospital. She also managed to make all the arrangements to get my poor father medivac'd out. My poor dad spent a couple of weeks in hospital in Palma before being flown by air ambulance back to the UK. Sad.

There was quite an interesting mixture of people living around Pollensa. There was the usual British retirees, everything from pub owners to retired generals. Also, quite a nice mix of nationalities so dinner parties used to be a real old social mish mash. There was also quite a variety of wealth. There were millionaires up on the hill and dirty old 'oilies' as well. Interesting.

One evening we had been invited to a retired German industrialist's house for a dinner party. We knew this couple quite well as the party circuit was relatively small and you tended to bump into the same people. The husband was quite elderly but his wife was a young, vivacious beauty. She had invited a strange mixture of people to this particular dinner party. There was a famous retired doctor and his wife from England, a retired army chap and his wife, then another two or three couples that we did not know. All 'terribly, terribly' and just a little bit staid. You could see our host and hostess trying to get this group to relax and mingle but the British stiff upper lip was having none of it.

Boy-oh-boy, I hate 'does' like that. After some strained conversation over our pre dinner drinks we eventually sat down to eat and the meal was delicious. About half way through dinner you could see that the guests were visibly relaxed and enjoying themselves. A short time later the table was an excited mix of conversation, laughter, jokes and everyone was getting on like a house on fire.

I whispered to our hostess – 'Okay – where was it?'

You know what she had done of course. She had 'spiked' the meal with hashish, I think it was in the Cumberland sauce. The whole table of very reserved English were as high as kites. The beauty of it was that they did not have a clue.

This same couple had another party earlier on, before we got to know them well. All the guests were British and we did our normal twenty to thirty minutes late – as is the British custom. When we got to the house there was a note on the gate

(You have to say this in a broad Prussian accent)

"Ze Party 'as bin cancelled due to late arrival of ze quests!!"

Wonderful, – and he meant it.

One more story before we move on. At our new 'finca' we had a large piece of land that had been an old olive grove. It was quite overrun and the whole area was full of weeds and brambles and was a right old mess. I rented one of those rotovator machines and for a whole year I cleared this land, weeded it, levelled it, put in an irrigation system and generally got it ready to plant some nice grass so that we could have rolling lawns between the olive trees. I thought that it would look quite nice.

We also had a gardener, Luciano, who used to come in to help twice a week. Luciano was quite an elderly gentleman but he worked well. Just after I got this piece of land prepared, and after a lot of hard work, I had to go away to Libya and it was one of those projects that dragged on and on. I think I must have been away for about two months. When I got back Luciano had planted the whole area with lettuce, onions and tomatoes. There was enough to start a market stall. I thought that I had explained to Luciano about the idea of planting grass but he obviously thought that this was a complete waste of good land. He was right of course but I still ended up throwing nearly all the tomatoes, onions and lettuce away. I didn't have the heart to tick the old man off. He had meant well. My grass had to wait another year.

By this time my marriage to Mia was showing strains. For quite a while we had been going through the pretences but the reality was that there was no passion and had not been for a long time. I was spending more and more time at work and I readily volunteered for some special projects up in Italy and Libya knowing full well that I would be away for quite an extended period.

I think the last straw for me was when I came home from Libya after an exceptionally long trip and I found that Mia had taken on a live-in house maid. That's as well as the Au Pair, mark you.

When I got home late that evening, Mia, the Au Pair and the new Live-in House maid were all sitting down together on the outside patio having dinner. I ended up serving them and acting 'Mine Host'. I had some pretty severe words after that little episode but the marriage was finished and we both knew it.

A few days later I came back from an afternoon of windsurfing to find Mia in bed feeling 'poorly'.

Oh dear – shame – 'Would you like one of the staff to come in and read to you?'

So we decided to go our separate ways.

We parted amicably enough but we did not bother to get divorced for several more years. There didn't seem to be too much point or rush. It was just a piece of paper.

# LIBYA

I had been in and out of Libya a few times on special projects, mainly well testing, over the last few years but my main assignment was still Algeria. All this changed in 1984 when Mr Gadafi and the US Government had some pretty serious differences of opinion and the US Government imposed a boycott on Libya. All Americans had to leave and we Brits were sent in to fill their positions. I was sent in as the boss of one of the southern regions around Whaha and Zelton. These are about eight hundred kilometres south of Benghazi. I had two operations bases to manage but had a wonderful crew and we had some fun. In fact in retrospect I enjoyed my work in Libya a lot. The Libyans were nice and we got on well with them.

The adventure of Libya was that there were hardly any roads. To get to any rig sites or well sites you literally just drove across the desert. There were routes across the desert such as The Barrel Route ( empty oil drum every five to ten kilometres), The Toilet Route ( some witty humourist had put a complete old toilet on top of one of the sand ridges), The Old Tyre Route, etc.. Driving there was fun and we would quite happily set out on our own to go one or two hundred kilometres over the open desert.

I arrived in Waha in style. On my first trip on this new assignment I got to Benghazi and spent a couple of days with the area supervisor seeing what they had in the way of materials and support for our operations. I needed to get down to the base at Waha but there were no planes and I did not know the route so I agreed to take a lift in the next supply truck heading that way. I strapped my kit bag behind the cab of the Kenworth truck and climbed in for the long run south. The driver was a Yugoslavian lad and he had obviously been doing this run for quite a while.

He knew every camp along the way and seemed to have friends in or near every village we went through.

Who said Libya was 'dry'? There was wine offered at every stop, home made beer, flash. It was amazing. Every stop we were made to feel welcome but I was just a bit concerned about the state of this Yugoslavian driver. If he kept going like this he would be as drunk as a skunk and we would never get to Waha.

We pulled into the base at Waha in the early evening. The lads there were expecting their new boss but they did not expect me to arrive in the cab of a Kenworth truck looking tired, dusty and sweaty. But that was life in the oilfield. There were no pretences or posing. Job to do, so let's get on with it.

I was commuting to Libya from Mallorca and used to spend four weeks in the desert followed by four weeks off in Mallorca, which worked out pretty good most of the time.

The only real hiccup we had was when Mr Ronald Reagan decided to bomb Tripoli and Benghazi. I was due to fly in on the day after the bombing but obviously that was going to have to go on 'hold'. Normally we would fly up from Waha into the main central base by the company's Pilatus Porter. Then catch a charter Fokker from our desert strip up to Tripoli. Apparently the day of the bombings our Pilatus was up in the air when the local air traffic controller suddenly told all aircraft to get out of the sky and to land immediately. The Pilatus had nowhere to land so he went down to ground level and weaved his way home between the sand dunes.

I came into the country about five days after the bombing and we had to go a round about route through Tripoli then on to Benghazi and from there by road down to Waha. I was amazed at the bomb damage. The US planes had hit everything. There were shrapnel marks all over the airport buildings and every plane on the ground had been hit. There were half planes, parts of planes, planes tipped on their sides. It was pretty impressive.

I did not see any damage outside the airports and it looked as if they had hit exactly what they wanted to hit.

After that, of course, everyone got a bit jumpy. The Libyans set up anti-aircraft guns all over the place. On the top of buildings, on flyovers, in palm groves and masses of them around the airports, of course. The Libyans still treated us all very politely and were still very friendly. They even made a special immigration facility for expats to speed up the formalities. Any poor Libyans returning to the country had to wait in long queues and were treated quite badly. We went straight through. No problems, no hassles.

By this time we also had armed guards down in Waha and a new barrier and gate going into the area. We had not asked for this. It was just suddenly there. These guards were not exactly la Crème de la Crème of the Libyan army by the way. They were old codgers who had been given a loaded AK47 and told to guard the gate. They were more afraid and worried than anyone. One evening I was driving back in the dark to Waha and had to stop at this gate for the guard to open it. You could see the poor bugger shaking. He came towards me with his gun aimed right at my head and I could see his nervous, twitching finger was on the trigger. This guy was not taking any chances of having his life shortened by some aggressive foreigner. When he got to the side of the Land Cruiser I had to smile disarmingly and do my Arabic greetings to put him at his ease. I know how to say it but I haven't got a clue how to write it, so just accept 'Arabic greeting'. I gently got hold of the barrel of his rifle and moved it off to the side. I felt like one of the hippy's from the 'Ban the Bomb' era or the demonstrations against the Vietnam war where they put flowers into the barrels of the guns that were confronting them.

'Give Peace a Chance'

The work in Libya was interesting and time passed quickly.

Meanwhile back in Mallorca on my days off, I am afraid I went a bit off the rails. Being on my own in the house meant there were no limits. I would party all night long and generally make a complete idiot of myself. I was bouncing into bed with a different lass every night and I was drinking far too much. Not a very satisfactory existence.

This actually went on for quite some time as I was assigned to Libya for two years. I did calm it down a bit but I was still drinking way too much. It was not bordering on alcoholism but there were a lot of times when I was drunk. I was not getting up in the morning and having a bevy. It was not that bad. It was just that the nights were long and I did not know when to stop.

Hey Ho – Another of life's lessons.

I was still very active and spent most of the days water skiing or wind surfing and I was in pretty good shape. Actually, I wasn't going to mention this, but then I thought – why not? The girls only told me a long time afterwards but they had voted me as the 'Best Body in Mallorca'. You see, I am still secretly quite proud of that. Actually, they probably meant the Best Body in Puerto Pollensa, or the Best Body on that 50 metre stretch of beach. But I was in good shape and very fit but I wasn't going to stay like that forever the way I was partying and drinking.

The last straw was when I drove off the road into a field on my way home one evening. I did not crash the car, I just came to my senses driving around in a field. This was getting silly. Time to get a grip and move on.

# CONGO

By this time I had done a couple of years in Libya and Halliburton asked me to go to Congo and get their operations there off the ground. This was going to be a Live-In contract and I would be living in Pointe Noire which is the main (and only) port on the coast. This Congo is not the old Belgian Congo by the way. It is the old French Congo which sits between Gabon and what was then Zaire.

(I wish they would stop changing the names of countries).

This was an eye opener. Dr Livingstone and all that. You could almost feel the presence of old explorers and adventurers. The Congo was not just poor, it was a derelict, desperate, sad place. Poverty and disease screamed at you wherever you went. It wasn't just the poverty that gave the place its air of doom and gloom. It was the oppressive humidity and the almost tangible smell of decay about the place. The Congo sits right up on the Equator and it has two seasons. The rainy season which has long hours of very hot sun interspersed with torrential downpours and some of the most impressive thunderstorms I have ever experienced. The dry season on the other hand is six months of overcast skies when you hardly ever see the sun. It seems the wrong way round but that's the way it is. I learnt to like it and years later I was to go back there with Joanne and we both liked it. Very different. Very basic. Extremes.

When I arrived in Congo, Halliburton had no operations running but some equipment had been transferred to Pointe Noire with the hope of securing some contracts. I was on my own, quite literally. There was only one other English speaking person in the whole place and he was the manager of a small supply boat company that had also recently moved in.

No way out of this one Trevor. Time to brush up on your old school French as you are not going to succeed here without it.

What follows was one of the most rewarding experiences in my life.

As I built up my contacts in Congo I could see that there was going to be some offshore activity and in order to secure any contracts I had to get organised and show that we could deliver. I hired two local lads from the village to help me with one of the bulk materials supply points down in the port. These two lads came from shacks in the village.

This was the reality of Africa. No electricity, no running water and sewage in the dirt streets. They were poor beyond poor, as were most of the Congolese. Leon and Johnny – my helpers. I gave them a fair wage and arranged for safety boots and coveralls for them. They were so proud. They would walk through their neighbourhood in their bright red coveralls, showing off and generally trying to make everyone jealous, – I am sure they succeeded.

We won a contract for AGIP – Yipee! We were off and running. Just me, Leon and Johnny. What a team!

That first year we barely made enough to pay for the rental of my house. But the next year we won more contracts with ELF and Amoco and we had some impressive revenues coming in. The third year was even better. All from next to nothing. Highly profitable and highly exciting.

We were all very proud and I would set revenue targets as an excuse to throw a celebration party for Leon, Johnny and their wives and families. It was fun and they were justifiably proud.

You know, years later I was up in Algeria again and was asked to go down to Pointe Noire to supervise on a blow out that they had offshore. When I got off the helicopter on the offshore barge there were Leon and Johnny. Leon was now an operator and he was more than proud. We were like long lost brothers. Lots of hugs and lots of photos taken.

They were successful. They had a good income and they

were living well. That was a miracle for Congo. I was proud of them.

The icing on the cake only happened about four years ago. Out of the blue I got an e-mail from Leon. He was working for Halliburton in Gabon as a Supervisor and he was being paid in US dollars and what advise could I give him on banking and investments. 'Could I please reply to his e-mail address'. Wonderful – what a lovely story.

The social life in Pointe Noire was quite interesting. There were quite a lot of French girls and the best way to learn a language is via the pillow. I must admit I found the French girls very refreshing. Their attitude to relationships and sex was completely open and unrestrained. They were sexy. There was an undercurrent of the erotic. There was none of the coy shyness of the English. I know that I am making some sweeping generalisations here but this is what I felt so you will just have to put up with it. I did not go bed hopping. Pointe Noire was so small that there was no way you could get away with that but there were no barriers. Ménages à trois and à quatre were not uncommon.

My first girlfriend there was a lovely French girl, Lisa, who taught at the local French School. It was a comfortable relationship. Surprisingly, she did not speak a word of English so it was French or die. We spent a lot of time together and went off on holiday to Kenya to explore the Masai Mara together. Comfortable. I think that I impressed her a bit as well as we had to get over the Congo river from Brazzaville to Kinshasa on our way to catch an Ethiopian airlines flight to Nairobi. That is easier said than done in Congo but I just arranged for a Cessna to pick us up in Brazzaville and fly us the short distance over the river to drop us on the tarmac in Kinshasa. No problem – easy. We did the same on the way back as well. We landed in Kinshasa and I just got the airport staff to phone across to Brazzaville and send 'my Cessna' to pick us up.

There is no limit to what this guy can do!

It was about this time in 1986 that I got a call to say that my father had died. Thankfully it was one of those sudden massive strokes. One minute he was sitting down in the lounge and the next minute he was on the floor and out.

By this time I had a secretary / general assistant in Congo and she was super. She had me out on a flight that same evening and I was up in North Yorkshire the following afternoon.

Shame – Dad was 74 at the time so he had had a good innings but I wish that he could have come out to visit some of the places I went to. We had actually been to many of the same places and I know that he would have enjoyed revisiting West Africa and Algeria.

Mum arranged a nice, quiet funeral service in the village church in Great Ayton but much to her surprise an enormous number of people turned up. The little church was bursting at the seams and there wasn't even enough room for all the people that came to pay their respects. It was standing room only. My father was a very well respected man and I think that Mum was very happy and proud to see such a huge crowd turn up for his funeral service.

Well done Dad.

After the service we had Dad cremated, as per his wishes.

Now here's a story that needs telling. I nearly forgot about this one.

Dad had requested that his ashes be spread over farmland up in the old village of Garrigill where he grew up. So Mum and I went down to the funeral place after the cremation to collect his ashes. I left Mum in the car and went inside to collect the ashes. The person in charge handed me a plastic sample bottle with Dad inside.

Hey – wait a minute. I can't hand this cheapy, nasty sample bottle to Mum.

This is terrible.

'Haven't you got an urn or something a little less vulgar?'

Damn it – I could rush into town and buy an earthenware pot or even a tea caddy. Anything was better than this plastic sample bottle.

But then what would you do Trev – decant Dad into a tea caddy? How would you explain the Sainsbury's Best Earl Grey label on Dad's remains. No we would have to live with the plastic sample bottle.

Apparently, if you want a special urn or other container you have to order it. Never having been through this situation before we did not know the 'fine print' on these arrangements. Actually, I was shocked. I hope that they have changed their policy on this by now.

Be that as it may. I popped Dad into the boot of the car and I drove Mum up to Garrigill where we walked up into a field at the back of the old farm. I left Mum to have her private moment and she stood there for quite a while before gently pouring the ashes over the coarse moorland grass. Hugs and tears and God speed Dad. Thanks.

I think that Mum was still in a bit of shock after all this, but she is a tough lady, and still is, and she braced herself, pulled her shoulders back and got on with life.

So back onto another aeroplane and back to the delights of Pointe Noire, Congo and Lisa.

Lisa and I had been together for about one year and we got on well so it came as a shock to both of us when I fell in love with someone else. This was one of those really 'In Love' things. I had not gone looking for it. It just happened.

Let me tell you the story.

By this time work in the Congo was becoming quite active and there were several new families moving into Pointe Noire. One family was a young French couple that I became friendly with. The sister of the husband came out to visit them. Annie.

She was absolutely drop dead gorgeous. Beautiful black hair and deep dark eyes and a body to die for. Annie was also one of those people who make a difference. She had grown up in French Guiana in South America where her father had worked for many years as an air traffic something or other. She and her family had explored the Amazon and had hiked and camped in the tropical forests around that area and in Cayenne. She was another of those adventurous Paula types that I am instantly attracted to.

Doomed Renwick lad – doomed is what you are!

It was not love at first sight and it did take a couple of days before we became a number.

Ahha – but what a number!

I had to go and explain myself to Lisa. That was not pleasant but it had to be done.

There is an interesting little side note on this episode. While I was 'in Love' with Annie my future wife and proper 'Love of my Life' was going through the same 'In Love' period with a chap in South Africa. Strange don't you think?

Annie's brother and sister–in–law were nice people and we were often invited there for dinner. They had rented a house and were waiting for their shipment of furniture to arrive from France. The wife was very excited about this as it was her first international posting and she had spent a long time and a lot of money choosing the furniture and everything was brand new from the sofas to the televisions and stereo system. Absolutely everything was 'straight out of the box'. You can see another disaster looming on the horizon, can't you ?

Sure enough the day came when their shipment was supposed to be delivered to the house and they asked me if I could be there to help. We waited and waited and after about three hours, round the corner comes this big truck with some enormous wooden boxes on the trailer behind it. The problem was, these boxes were flattened. Absolutely squashed flat. The poor wife actually screamed when she saw them and then broke down in hysterics.

There was not one piece of furniture intact. The whole lot was a jumble of splintered furniture and smashed appliances. Oh dear me.

They had not specified that their shipment should be loaded in a container and the shipping company had just piled freight on top of these boxes until they were flattened.

The hassle was that you could not buy decent furniture in Pointe Noire and it took them ages to get the money from the insurance, so they ended up living on broken beds and smashed sofas for several months whilst it all got sorted out.

While on this subject about furniture I must tell you this other funny story about my own attempts to purchase some decent beds. When I got to Congo I just lived in a rented furnished house. It was easier that way and being single at the time there was not pressure to have any fancy sofas or dinning room suites. But – a bed is important. It must be comfortable.

The bed I had in that furnished house was awful so I made arrangements with a local merchant to get a couple of new beds for the house. Imported beds. I did not want any of those locally made things – Good imported beds was what I wanted and that was what I ordered.

Weeks went by – no beds. Patience Trevor lad. I pestered the merchant. He assured me that they would arrive soon. Another week or two went by – Nothing.

Eventually, I got a call to say that the new beds had arrived and they would be delivered that afternoon. Great.

Yes, they did arrive that afternoon and they were awful. The mattresses were just a mass of hard lumps. The springs were nearly bursting through the outer materials. They were terrible. I got hold of the merchant,

'What the bloody hell is this. These are terrible. I though I made it clear that I wanted good imported beds and mattresses'.

He bent down and showed me the label on the mattress 'Made in Cameroon'.

He had followed my instructions. They were imported all right, but from Douala.

Another lesson – be sure your instructions are clear and specific.

The danger of assumptions.

So time passed happily enough. The work was good, I was in love and Pointe Noire was not too bad. But of course there has to be a spanner in the works somewhere.

I had moved to the Congo in about 1986 and had been there for about three years. The operations were successful and there was a good team working there now.

Halliburton considered that my job was done there and it was time to move me to a new area of operations. Back to Algeria.

We had closed our operations in Algeria in 1984 and I had been the last person to leave Hassi Messaoud. We had re-exported all the main equipment to Valencia in Spain and all that was left were some odds and ends. I had hired a crew to build a wire fence around the equipment that was left and then went down to the hardware store and bought a padlock and chain and locked the whole lot up. Climbed into my Chevy and headed north to Algiers.

In the intervening years Halliburton had negotiated a new contract and were ready to move back into the country and get the operations going again. This is what I was good at. Go in somewhere on my own and get things going. It was exciting, lean and mean and not bogged down in the bureaucracy of established projects.

So the call came. "Trevor we want you back into Algeria as Operations Manager. When can you be there?"

It was move time. Annie and I discussed it and she agreed to come with me.

But – there was a 'but' here again. I could see that she was thinking hard about this and the fact that moving to Algeria and living in Algiers with me was quite a major commitment and was not an easy decision. On top of that I was not a young stud any more. This was 1989 and I was 43 years old (a bloody good 43 I might add). Annie was still just 29. Ummmm. Think about that for a while Trevor. Were you really being fair?

Anyway, we packed everything up and I headed for Algiers. Annie was going to France to visit her parents and would join me when I had a house and had settled in.

I went via Tunis first to visit my boss and to look after the operations in Tunisia while he and his family took a vacation. I phoned Annie from Tunis and could tell immediately that something was wrong. She had decided not to come to join me in Algiers. Final. Finish. Gone.

Damn but I was sad. I was in a real state for quite a while. Back to the usual oilfield method of coping with crisis and stress – copious amounts of alcohol – again – and bonking everything in sight!

# Back to Algeria for the second time

It was exciting to be back in Algeria again. Halliburton had secured a major contract and there was a lot of work to be done. There was a very small team living in Algiers but we all knew the country well and knew how to operate there. I was living in a tiny fishing village, Tamentafourst, which is on the east side of the bay of Algiers. Basic but fun.

It was quite a struggle to get set up as Algeria modelled itself on French bureaucracy and as a measure of efficiency they multiplied the bureaucratic nightmare to an unbelievable level. Getting gas bottles was a cracker. You can't have gas bottles unless you return empty ones. But I don't have any empty bottles. I have just arrived. Then you can't have any gas bottles. Same with beer. No empty bottles – no beer. Quite a struggle.

I don't know if you have spent a lot of time in any of these older socialist countries but it is quite amazing. How they ever get anything done is a miracle. The whole system seems to work at a negative level. No you can't do this without that, and you can't do that without this, and since you are a foreigner you can't do either this or that! We had the same in the Congo.

But there are always ways round these problems. Make your own official looking rubber stamps. That's always a good one. In fact way back in the Congo I got stuck with some import of materials as the customs said that the papers had not been stamped correctly by the officials of the country of origin. I got a newish British coin and using an ink pad I stamped all the documents with a ten pence piece. There – that's better – problem over.

I spent a lot of the first few months belting around Algeria, from Algiers to Hassi Messaoud, Hassi Messaoud up to Mostaganem on the coast, back again. One of the things I had to do was to plan a suitable route through the Atlas mountains and down into the desert to avoid any low bridges or any routes that could not take this large number of very heavy and very big equipment. That was interesting as I had to check the height of every bridge and power line on the proposed route to ensure that our trucks would go under them. It was quite hectic but we were busy and I needed this frenzy of activity to get over my lost love.

Halliburton was importing a huge spread of very fancy equipment for this new contract and I spent a lot of time in the port of Mostaganem getting everything ready to clear customs as quickly as possible. I rented a small house in the town that was more than basic. It was rough. But with a good team and working hard and long hours, who cares.

The day eventually arrived when the specially chartered Roll On /Roll Off ship arrived from the US with all our new equipment. That was fun – masses and masses of new, bright red toys to play with. Then the real hard work started. The contract stated that we would only go on contract and start to be paid when all the equipment was down south in Hassi Messaoud and ready to begin operations. In fact we managed this in an amazing record time of ten days from the time that the ship docked. That is rocking on, I'm telling you. I am rather proud of that one.

The first few jobs we did under that contract involved the usual start up glitches and small problems but by and large they ran smoothly enough. The jobs themselves are quite complex. It is called Fracturing and this is a method for increasing the production of oil or gas from a well. Basically, what you do is pump into a well at very high pressure to crack open the rock way down in the producing formation. This can be anything from 5,000 to 20,000 feet underground. Once the rock has been cracked by this huge pressure from our pumps we keep the crack open by pumping at a very high rate and then we inject high strength beads, or proppants, into this crack to create a highly permeable artificial formation. The oil or gas is no longer trapped and has an easy unrestricted path to the well bore and up to surface. That was a huge over-simplification as it is quite a high tech operation and if any of our engineers ever read this they will probably shoot me but I hope it gives you the picture.

Obviously, with all these pumps and mixing equipment we need a quite a big team to run them and although we had a core of technical people permanently assigned to Algeria we had to get some of the pump operators and other staff from the US, as and when we needed them. For many of them it would be their first time outside the USA and I suspect that for some of them it was their first time away from their home town. Their knowledge of geography is quite shocking.

I had one chap come up to me shortly after arriving in Hassi Messaoud.

'Trevor, where am I ?'

'You are in Hassi Messaoud'.

'Yea Trevor, but where's that?'

'Hassi Messaoud is in Algeria'.

'Yea Trevor, but where's Algeria?'.

'Algeria is in North Africa'.

'Yea Trevor but where's ....... ' Ahhaaa – I give up!

Another cracker happened on the very first evening of the very first team's arrival in Hassi Messaoud. It had been a long day and I was tired. The team had arrived from the USA in the evening and after the usual hassles of getting them settled in and making sure that they knew what to do and what not to do, they had been fed and watered and instructed to be up and about by four in the morning to get all the equipment checked out. I eventually managed to get to bed at about eleven at night. I was in a deep sleep when at about one o'clock in the morning I was woken up by a knocking on my door. What on earth is this?

'Hang on'.

Knock, Knock.

'Hang on I'm coming'.

I went to the door and opened it to find a huge, six and a half foot tall, Texan staring down at me.

The guy was built like the side of a house. Huge. Broad shoulders. Tough guy. The very picture of American masculinity, strength and virility.

'Trevor, my pillow's too hard'.

I am not making this up. I am not usually lost for words, but I was then. Amazing.

Life in Algiers was good but only if you knew where to go. It is not exactly a tourist destination and there are very few facilities where expats can go to relax. The majority of the expats in Algiers were embassy staff and I soon got to find out where the old British Club was hidden under the library of the old British Council building. Normally I am not too keen on British Clubs. The ones I had known in the Middle East were full of the old Empire types – Old England's not finished yet – sitting under their sun umbrellas with their Pimms. I was always amazed at how much 'whinging' and complaining goes on at these British Clubs.

Maybe they have changed by now. I hope so.

The British Club in Algiers was not like that at all. It was really a disused basement that a group of enterprising folks at the embassy had turned into a bar. That's all it was – a bar. A place to gather. It was the only place that people from all the embassies could meet and congregate and generally relax. It was a bit rough so the ambassadors and their families were rarely seen down there. So that was my watering hole in the evenings. We used to have quite a few visitors at the club as it became known to some of the overland tours that were still running in those days. Some evenings we would find an old Bedford ex-army truck parked outside the club with "London to Cape Town" stencilled on the side.

For the first time I was able to invite my Mum to come out to visit one of the countries I worked in. She needed a break. Actually this was to become quite a ritual as I moved from country to country. Years later Joanne and I were on our way to Venezuela and when Mum rang up one day we told her where we were going.

'Oh wonderful', she said, 'a new country to explore'
We hadn't even invited her yet.
I'll tell you more about that later on.

So Mum flew into Algiers and I got her settled into my little house in the fishing village of Tamentafourst. She loved it. I am not quite sure why as it was really basic but love it she did. There was a bit of a hiccup while she was there as I had to go belting off to Tunis or London, I can't remember which, for a meeting so I had to ask my current Philippino girlfriend to move into the house and look after Mum while I was away for a couple of days. Not sure if Mum appreciated that but it was unavoidable.

As soon as I got back we piled into my big Chevy Suburban and headed south for Hassi Messaoud. Up over the Atlas mountains, through the gorges and then the long run south on the high plateau, before descending into the desert. It was a long drive so we broke the trip in Guardia which has the

166

old legionnaire's fort converted into a hotel. Not a very good hotel but Guardia is a lovely little desert town with a wonderful market so it is always worth a visit.

Mum loved it. It was all a new experience for her.

Next morning off we set for Hassi Messaoud which is another 300 kms further south. There was a mother of a sand storm blowing and by the time we got to Ouagla you could hardly see the road. Another new experience for Mum.

At this time we were still using a very basic hotel in Hassi as our living base. The manager of the hotel put on a special cocktail party and a special dinner for Mum and she was suitably impressed. She was being treated like visiting royalty and was lapping it up.

When she went to bed I forgot to tell her about the cockroaches. She couldn't understand why her little metal frame bed was in the middle of the room so she pushed it back against the wall. Ha, Ha. She told me she woke up in the night to find half a dozen cockroaches climbing over her. These cockroaches are not the little ones that skitter around Europe. These bloody things have thrown their rider and are galloping around with saddles on their back. They are huge.

Anyway, Mum was absolutely enthralled with the desert and she still says that was one of her most favourite holidays.

A year later I sent her on a cruise in the Caribbean as a spoily present. She is polite about it but it is quite obvious that she was bored to death and did not really enjoy it. So that gives you some kind of insight into her personality. A good lady.

After a few days in the south we drove back up to Algiers by a different route, up through the mountains to the east of the country. The mountain passes on that route are pretty hairy so I think she was glad to get back to the safety of my little house in Tamentafourst.

Nice adventure for her. She often tells us about the reaction of some (most?) of her friends in Great Ayton when she got back. When she tries to explain where she has been a blank look comes over their faces.

'Where have you been Betty?'

'On holiday in the Sahara'

'Oh how nice – did you know that Mrs. Smith's cat got run over'

Shame.

Meanwhile in Algiers I was just about to make a big mistake. I started to go out with 'Fatal Attraction'. I'll just call her 'Fatal' from now on as it simplifies things. I am not going to go into any details on this so you will just have to use your imagination.

As an expat in these type of countries you are part of a very small group of people and there is a very refreshing acceptance of everyone and everyone's little quirks and personality traits. You do not have any choice so you learn very quickly to accept people as they are and you learn to appreciate the good side of people and ignore any less attractive aspects of a person's personality.

Warts and all. That's my excuse and I am sticking to it.

Fatal worked for the British Ambassador and lived in the residence. Actually it gave me the opportunity to be invited to quite a few dinner parties and other functions. Some of the more formal ones were quite an eye opener. The Queen's birthday is celebrated at every British Embassy world wide and all the local dignitaries and government officials are invited. This is a very puccka do and everyone is in their finery. In Algiers the reception was always held on the lawns in front of the residence and there would be a hundred or more guests standing out there in the burning summer sun sipping champagne. The Embassy always has a piper flown in from the UK and he is up on the upper balcony of the residence playing his bagpipes. It really is quite an impressive function and all paid for by the good old British tax payer. No expense spared.

In 1992 there was a Coupe d'Etat in Algeria and the military seized power. That was interesting. One of our operations teams had just finished a campaign in the south and I was trying to get them flown back to the USA for their break. The flights up from Hassi Messaoud were being cancelled right, left and centre and there was an overtone of tension in the air around the country. If I could not get these lads, and there were about twenty of them, onto a flight to Algiers to catch their connections the only option left was for them to drive up in convoy. So we arranged that they would drive up and that I would meet them at the bottom of the Atlas Mountains where the mountains come down to the coastal plain. We worked out that if they left Hassi at five the next morning they should be coming down out of the mountains at about five that evening and so we arranged that I would meet them at a prearranged spot and escort them into town to their hotel.

Best laid plans of mice and men.

Sure enough at five that next evening I was waiting at the foot of the mountains at the end of one of those beautiful deep gorges when I saw this convoy of about six Chevy's heading my way. Everyone was fine so I told them to follow me into town.

We could not get into town. There were tanks and barricades and road blocks all over the place. Okay – Plan 32B –"Follow me by the back roads to my house in Tamentafourst. I have plenty of rooms and beds and mattresses. You can all doss down there for the night".

It worked – I got them all set up in the house and then arranged for them to go to the local village restaurant to be fed and, make themselves at home. I was going to drive into Algiers by another route to see what was going on and to see Fatal. I would be back in a couple of hours. Ha Ha

As I got closer into Algiers I could see row after row of tanks and armoured personnel carriers in the side streets. Also ambulances – lots of them, just parked down side streets – waiting. What in heaven's name is going on ?

I got as far as the ambassador's residence and that is as far as I got that evening. The whole bloody place erupted. There was gunfire all over the city and tracer bullets streaking through the night sky. It was quite impressive actually. I was safe enough at the residence so I just stayed there.

The next morning it seemed to have calmed down a bit so I headed home. I managed to get through the road blocks but by now there were tanks and troops at every intersection.

The lads staying in my house had had a wonderful night and they had cleaned out my stock of booze totally. They had a wonderful view across the bay of the mayhem going on in Algiers and had stayed up most of the night watching the fireworks. So I gathered up this bleary eyed, hung over team and we set off for the airport.

Considering the circumstances I was amazed that they actually managed to get on the flights and get out of there.

It was a strange few months that followed. The gun fire would erupt most nights but the daylight hours were calm. It was as if I was living in two different worlds.

Living in Tamentafourst was getting a bit dodgy. I was miles out of town and I was the only foreigner living in that whole area. The last straw was the lawlessness at night. I was broken into and robbed three times and one evening there was a gun battle in the street just outside the house. I was actually ordered by Halliburton to get out of there and move to a safer area in Algiers, which I did quite happily.

The house I moved to was really quite special. It was on a cliff top overlooking the whole city of Algiers. It was quite beautiful. Also had nine bedrooms and five bathrooms, I might add. It was a fantastic place for parties and receptions so it got well used. It was also a good vantage point to watch the night time activities as the various factions fought it out in the streets and suburbs. You could clearly see the tracer rounds and sound of gunfire was constant but I never felt threatened. The only precaution you had to take was to stay behind the parapet in case any stray rounds or ricochets came your way.

It was as if you were watching it on a big screen in a cinema and you were not really there. Weird.

The situation went on like that for some months with the gunfire gradually diminishing but at the same time the threat from extremists increased. We continued to work as normal but had to vary our route to the office and come and go at odd times to avoid establishing a pattern.

There was also a curfew imposed by the authorities and that led to some pretty silly curfew parties. Since you could not go home until dawn these parties went on all night. Really silly.

Unfortunately, we had to close the British Club as it would have been an easy target for extremists and we were too vulnerable there. As far as I know it has never re-opened and remains closed to this day. Shame.

I enjoyed my time in Algeria on that assignment. It was exciting, it was fun and the project was a super success. We had explored and camped out in parts of the desert I had never seen before and had lived in the busy, bustling noisy city of Algiers and had experienced some of its pain. Time to move on.

I am good at getting things up and running. Leave me alone to get on with things and I am fine. Unfortunately, as a project or contract becomes more and more successful, more and more interference comes in from head office. More controls, more reports, more restrictions. Not my cup of tea.

A new manager was appointed and I was informed that I was to be sent to South Africa to manage Halliburton's business there as well as in Namibia, Botswana, Zimbabwe and Mozambique. I was told later on that the Halliburton management realised that I had been in some pretty awful places for a long, long time and that this posting was my reward. I am not sure how true that is but it made me feel pretty good. It also hinted that such a soft posting was not going to last too long.

There is a bit of a funny story attached to this posting. About a year before Fatal and I wanted to have a holiday. It was a toss up between South Africa and the Caribbean.

Eany meany miny mo.

The Caribbean won. Thank God as I would have spent a bunch of money going on holiday to a country I was now going to live in.

One more strange thing – While on this holiday in the Caribbean we went to explore the Grenadine Islands, where we chartered a yacht to sail across and have a look at Princess Margaret's and Mick Jagger's island of Mustique, which is just a few hours sailing from the island of Bequia. We stayed in Bequia for about three days and were then going on to Barbados. As we were walking to the jetty to catch the ferry back to Saint Vincents I noticed a familiar pair of skinny ankles ahead of me. There was Annie with her boyfriend. Yes – that Annie. They had sailed across the Atlantic from West Africa and there they were, taking a break in Bequia. Amazing – It kind of knocked me sideways to tell the truth as she was still in my heart and I still hadn't quite got over her. Hey Ho

We had a couple of beers with them and they invited us to stay but I felt awkward and we had a flight to catch in St

Vincent so we parted with a peck on the cheek, I climbed on board the ferry and left.

In hind sight I think that chance meeting helped me to close that chapter of my life.

Right where was I?

Ah yes,- leaving Algeria

I said farewell to everyone including Fatal and after a short break in Mallorca I set off for Cape Town to meet my wife, whose name I did not know yet.

# South Africa

I don't like living in hotels but you really do not have much choice when you move into a country. You have to get your bearings, decide where you want to live and you also have to wait for your shipment of household goods and furniture to catch up with you.

As I had taken a vacation my shipment was not far behind me and South Africa is efficient and civilised. I quickly arranged to rent a house in Bantry Bay in Cape Town looking out over the sea and within a few days my shipment was there, cleared and delivered. What a wonderful, refreshing experience after the hassles and stupidity and corruption of some of the other countries I had been to.

Someone who had read through a draft of this little book said, (in a childish voice)

"Does he get the Girl? Does he get the Girl?"

Well – yes, he does and it is a nice story. Here goes.

When I learnt that I was leaving Algeria for South Africa, a friend of mine who was working in Algeria working for Neste Oy (The Finnish Oil Company) and who had been born and educated in old Rhodesia asked me if I would do him a favour. He had an old girlfriend who lived somewhere in Green Point in Cape Town and would I try to locate her and give her a letter. Of course. My pleasure.

So after I got settled in at my new house in Bantry Bay I started my little search to locate this lass, Erica, to whom the letter was addressed. I soon found the correct street and eventually the right house and I rang the doorbell. Erica came to the door and I explained that I was a perfect stranger but Roger had asked me to deliver this letter from him.

'Come in, come in, welcome'.

Erica could not have been more kind or hospitable. She offered me a drink and we sat and chatted and I told her about Algeria and what her old friend Roger was doing. It was a very pleasant afternoon. I explained that it was my first time in South Africa and I was still feeling my way around and did not know the area very well.

Erica promised to invite me round for dinner in the near future which was another nice gesture.

What I didn't know, until quite some time later, was that as soon as I left Erica picked up the phone and called Joanne.

"I have just met your husband," she declared.

I can imagine Joanne's response which would have been along the lines of 'go forth and get multiplied'. 'Nothing more to do with men,' etc,.

There was no positive reaction of 'Oh how nice, when can I meet him.'

Totally – No, Negative, Never. What part of 'no' don't you understand?

But Erica saw the match and she surreptitiously planned and schemed.

So the day came about a week later when I got a call from Erica inviting me for dinner at her house at such and such a time. She was very explicit about the time that I should be there. Okay – lovely thanks.

So I got there and was relaxing at an outside table having a glass of nice cold white wine when the doorbell goes and Erica ushers in a tall, red haired, elegant beauty in a bright, flame red jacket and long black trousers.

"Trevor, I'd like to introduce you to Joanne Wade. Joanne, this is Trevor Renwick'.

All the usually pleasantries. Joanne was not one of those shy little things. She had been a very successful business woman and she was not shy of coming forward. She intrigued me. All that confidence all that energy, all that beauty. And you could also tell that she had experienced some of the rough and tumble of life. She had fine scars on the right side of her face after going through a car windscreen at 21 years old. I hardly noticed but the overall impression was one of a very special, sexy, clever, beautiful woman.

At this point you have got to remember that both of us had been through a disastrous love affair in the not too distant past. Myself with Annie and Joanne with Andre. Neither of us wanted to go through that again. Neither of us was consciously out there looking for a partner. But the electricity was there flowing between us. We spent that very first evening, verbally skirting each other like two wrestlers pairing up for a fight.

Yes, Erica was right, but both of us were shying away.

We parted that evening with a promise that Joanne would show me round some of the wine farms in the region – sometime in the future. No dates, no arrangements made. Just a promise of something in the future. Not even phone numbers exchanged.

But some little seed had been sown somewhere.

I was having a house warming party at my new house so I thought that it would be nice to invite Erica, her husband and Joanne so I wrote the invitations and dropped them off at Erica's house. There was no answer at the door, so I just slipped the invite through the letter box.

I had my party and had all the local Halliburton people there but there was no sign of Erica or Joanne. Hey Ho – maybe it wasn't to be – let's just forget about it.

What I did not know was that Erica had gone away and she didn't even get my invite until a week after the party.

About ten days later, out of the blue, I got a call from Joanne.

Would I like to visit some of the wine farms with her.

Yes – lovely – meet in her house in Paarl and we would go on from there.

Which is what we did. We had a lovely lunch out at Del Aire wine estate where Joanne knew the owner, Storm, and we were treated as special guests and long lost friends. It was super and it later became one of our favourite places.

Then disaster struck.

Fatal appeared out of the blue in South Africa and made herself at home in my house and settled in to stay. Oh dear me.

I have to admit that I was a bit of a chicken on this as I should just have thrown her out and told her to go back to the UK but since Joanne and I had nothing really going yet, I didn't. Shame on you lad.

I actually rang Joanne and apologised that I would not be able to see her for a while which was a silly cowardly thing to do.

Joanne played on my mind. I was hoping that Fatal would just give up and go away but she didn't. I made her sleep in the spare room and was quite rude to her but still she stayed. Just which part of 'No' don't you understand?

It was Joanne who had the guts to try to move things along and she rang me one day and invited me to Paarl for a Sunday afternoon barbeque. I explained that I had this girl staying with me but Joanne just told me to bring her along.

By this time the unspoken messages between Joanne and I were getting stronger and stronger and we ended up with quite a passionate kiss in her kitchen when nobody was looking.

This is crazy. How on earth do I get rid of Fatal?

I invited Joanne for lunch at Del Aire but told her that I would be with friends. So I invited another male friend and took him and Fatal along to this wine farm in the hope that Fatal might latch on to him. Joanne and I were a bit naughty on this one as we just left them both there after lunch and we went off together for a run in my little sports car down to another wine farm to buy some of their nice rose wine. Pink Stuff as Jo called it.

It was all getting a bit messy.

In the mean time other friends of Joanne in Paarl had seen the potential match and were scheming away behind the scenes to bring us closer together. I was invited to a wedding as Joanne's partner and we danced and laughed and were definitely just a stone's throw from becoming a 'number'. I was even seen to put my hand under the back of her bright red jacket as we danced. Ahhha – this did not go unnoticed by the match makers and gossip columnists in Paarl. The famous Jo has something going on here!

I think it was that evening that I moved out from my house in Bantry Bay and just left Fatal there with instructions to pack up and move out. Eventually I had the guts to be firm.

She still didn't go. It became really silly. I gave notice on the house rental agreement and started to move all my stuff out. Joanne was quite concerned as Fatal was a bit of an unknown quantity and it could have gone from plain silly to downright dangerous. Joanne would not let me go there on my own and Sean, Joanne's son, would go there with me to collect items to make sure that I came back in one piece.

Bloody Hell – what a mess.

Hey Ho – anyway apart from a few work related trips Jo and I have been together ever since.

We went everywhere together and a few months later we went up to England so that Jo could meet my Mum. I had to attend a meeting in London so we both flew up there (and joined the five mile high club on the way – naughty children) and stayed at the Harrington Hall in West London. After a lovely dinner we were going up to our room in the lift and I proposed marriage there and then in the lift. I think we were on the 4th floor so in the few seconds that it took for the lift to go from the ground floor to the 4th floor I had proposed to Jo, and she had accepted. Isn't life wonderful!

We were like a couple of silly school kids. We ordered a bottle of champagne to be sent up to the room and then proudly told the room service chap that we had just become engaged.

'Oh, how nice', he said, without batting an eyelid.

After my meetings we took a few days off and went up to see Mum in North Yorkshire. We arranged to take her with us and do a little tour of the Lake District, which Jo had never seen. We kept our little secret until our first evening at the Eden Hall close to Ullswater. We sat Mum down in the bar area before dinner. I ordered a bottle of champagne and then we told her that we were going to get married. Glasses were raised, toasts given and we were one happy bunch. I think a little tear may have appeared in my eyes. I am a bit emotional about things like that.

Joanne and I got married at 11.00 am on 11th November 1994 in a beautiful, tiny slaves' chapel in the grounds of the Grand Roche Hotel in Paarl. The chapel can only hold ten people so the invitation list was purposely restricted to close friends. Mum flew down for the occasion and it was really very special. We had a harpist from the Cape Town Symphony Orchestra playing just outside this tiny chapel and with that and the setting it was really a very special ceremony. There was not a dry eye in the whole place. Erica was there and John and

Leslie, who had all contributed to bringing us together, were among this very small, special group.

The only person who had played a major part in this who was missing was Roger who had given me the letter to deliver from Algeria.

So there we are. I love that story. From being handed a letter in the middle of the Sahara desert to saying 'I do' in a tiny chapel in Paarl, South Africa. Wonderful.

Thank you Roger.

Jo and I spoilt ourselves. We had two honeymoons shortly after this. The first was to a property we had bought with eleven other people up on the West Coast of South Africa. This is up near Lamberts Bay which is about three hours drive north of Cape Town, if you know the area. There is absolutely nothing up there except for beautiful white beaches, dolphins, whales, porcupines and jackals. Wonderful. Six kilometres of private beach with not another soul in the world for miles around. We have a rusty, thirty year old caravan parked behind the sand dunes and that was our base. No need for clothes, cooking over an open fire and watching the magnificent night sky. The sky is so clear there that it feels as if you can reach out and touch the stars sometimes. Counting meteorites and satellites and listening to the background noise of the crashing waves. Magic.

We had a wonderful experience there with a wild jackal. We would cook our evening meal over the open fire and sit there watching the flames flicker as we ate. Jo noticed him first. There was a movement in the edge of the low bush scrub off to the side of the camp site. So we threw the bone of a lamb chop in that direction and sure enough there he was. He darted in and picked up the bone and high-tailed it back into the safety of the bushes. Another bone. The same.

The next night we threw the bones only about a metre or so outside the light from the camp fire.

In he came again. Then a bit closer, and a bit closer, until he was picking up the bones from within a metre of where we were sitting. On the third night he was eating out of our hands. Seriously. What a marvellous experience.

By the fifth night he became a pest and would dash into the camp site and push the pots and pans around looking for food.

Our second honeymoon was a couple of months later when we took a holiday in the Maldives.

I should mention here that I am not a very good passenger on an aircraft. I have a very vivid imagination. When I was younger flying had never bothered me but the more I flew the worse I got and I do a lot of flying. When you come in to land at Malé, which is the capital of the Maldives, you come in over the sea obviously. They have built the airport on the island with the runways sticking way out into the sea. I don't mind coming in to land on the sea if I am in a seaplane but when I am in an airliner with wheels I want to see some indication of land or a runway as we come in. Landing at Malé all you see is the sea. You are getting lower and lower and still all you can see is the sea. It is literally only at the very last second, just before the Dunlops hit the tarmac, that you see the runway. It is quite unnerving.

We had purposely chosen a very small island to stay on, quite a way from the beach to beach marble monstrosities that have been built for the tourists nearer to the main island. Our little island was way out in the less inhabited group of islands to the north and it was a good three hour boat trip to get there. We had a wooden cabin built on stilts in the beautiful turquoise tropical waters. Flowers and petals on the bed every night. Yes – I think we might go back there again.

Jo was a good swimmer but as she had suffered from asthma

when she was young she was not comfortable putting her head under water. So we had spent weeks training in our pool at home where she got used to diving under water and using a snorkel and mask. I was proud of her. After a spluttering, apprehensive start she was diving down the deep end, picking up coins that I placed there to get her used to being underwater. Very good girl.

We rented a couple of diving masks and snorkels and some flippers and we would walk down some wooden steps under our cabin, straight into the warm waters of the Indian Ocean. There were some nice coral reefs just a few meters out so I would hold Jo's hand and we would swim out to the reef together to explore and to watch the dazzling show of tropical fish darting to and fro amongst the coral. Idyllic.

Jo was getting more and more confident every day and she would happily drift over the coral watching the antics of the fish – Until – Yep, here comes another disaster.

We had both swum out to a particular part of the reef where the water was quite shallow. I would guess that there was only about five or six feet from the top of the coral to the surface. I had drifted off to one side when I saw the flash and frenzied splashing of Jo's bright yellow flippers.

Whoosh – she was off. She was going at the speed of light towards the shore. There was a bow wave in front of her she was going so fast. What in heavens name is going on? I eventually caught up with her and she gasped out her story. What had happened is that as she drifted over this reef a huge moray eel had come out of its hole right underneath her belly. I had not even seen this beast but Jo assured me that it was a monster.

I had also told her that she need not worry about sharks as this was shallow water, etc., etc.. Not exactly true but there is no need to make a nervous swimmer any more nervous. Sure enough we did not see a single shark – until the last evening. Every evening there was a little ceremony in front of the small bar on the beach. One of the lads from the hotel would go into the water to feed the sting rays. These rays knew exactly when it was time for their food and you would see their large dark shapes gliding through the clear water every evening as they headed for the waters in front of the bar. As soon as their food was offered they would mass around the poor chap feeding them and try to climb up his legs and generally stir things up quite a bit.

We had watched this little ceremony almost every evening as we sat and enjoyed our sun downers. It was interesting and nice. – But on the last night, as this chap was feeding the rays, there were several very fast movements in the water a few meters from him. You could not see what kind of fish these were as they were going so fast, but soon it was clear. Sharks. But only little small ones I told Jo. I must admit they were probably only about a meter long but that was enough for Jo. Thank God we only saw them on our last night or I would never have got her into that water. You lied you bounder! You told me that there would not be any sharks!

We had a lovely time there and at the end of our stay we took a seaplane back to the main island to catch our return flight to J'Burg. We had to wait about five hours on one of the main islands and they had arranged a day room at the hotel there so we could relax and rest before take off. I was horrified at what they had done to that island. It really was shore to shore marble. I know that those islands are small but that was ridiculous. It bore no resemblance to a tropical island. Thank heavens we had chosen well and decided to stay on one of the out of the way places.

My work in South Africa was fairly straightforward. The operations were well established before I even got there so there were not too many hassles. Unfortunately, that posting is perhaps a bit too soft for some people and I am afraid that some of the lads working there were spending a bit too much time staring into a bottle, if you see what I mean. I had to get a couple of lads moved on as they were not doing us, or themselves, any good.

One of the highlights of that assignment was Namibia. There were a few oil companies interested in some offshore exploration there and so we spent quite a bit of time in Windhoek and Walvis Bay meeting these customers and trying to secure some contracts, which we did. Next step was to set up some operations and support structure in Walvis Bay. That was interesting. I got an old friend of mine, Keith, to come in to run the Namibia operations and then it was time to arrange for some housing for Keith and his team. Joanne had come up with me so we decided that it would be better if Joanne organised the rental of suitable housing, as if I had tried to arrange it they would have realised that this was oil related and the price would have shot up. I just left Jo to it and she came back as proud as punch. She had rented a beautiful, fully furnished house in Langstrand, between Walvis bay and Swakopmund for the princely sum of $ 150 per month. I think this must have been the cheapest staff house that Halliburton has ever rented anywhere. The guys loved it as well, which is the most important thing. Whenever we visited Namibia Jo and I would stay with the lads at this staff house and it was a good team and we were all working hard and having fun.

Keith was putting in a lot of extra time to get these operations running and I owed him quite a bit of time off. We negotiated that if I flew his family across from the USA to stay with him then we would be even. That was easy to do in those days but I doubt that it would be accepted nowadays. Anyway, Keith's wife, Jody and their two kids flew across to Cape Town where we put them up. Keith came down from Namibia and after a couple of days of sightseeing they set off for Walvis Bay.

Joanne and I joined them up there about a week later and they were having a high old time. There was one evening we had with them there which we will always remember. We had been out for dinner and when we got back to the house in Langstrand it was one of those gorgeous clear evenings where the stars and the Milky Way were almost bright enough to read by. It was magic and then as the waves were breaking on the shoreline there were the most intense flashes of phosphorescence that I have ever seen in my life. It was as if there was a giant turquoise searchlight under the sea running along under each wave. We all ran down to the sea and splashed around in the waves. The phosphorescence glowed under your feet in the sand and stuck to your legs when you went in the sea. It was quite magical.

Jo and I took advantage of these trips to explore Namibia a bit, but you know, even now we have still a lot left to explore. We will go up there again soon. Looking forward to that.

# MOZAMBIQUE

Part of my area of responsibility while in South Africa was Mozambique. There was not really a lot going on there but there were some plans afoot for some gas development in a place called Pande which was way up north of Maputo (previous Lourenco Marques – why do they keep changing these names?). Halliburton was invited to tender for some of the work but it was decided that we would do this as a kind of joint venture with an Australian drilling outfit. You know – a whole package of all the services and products they would need from a single source type of thing. So the plan was that I would fly over to Melbourne and sit down with these guys and put together our offer and then go back to Mozambique to present it. No big deal.

You probably think that we super high powered oil field executives fly around in the lap of luxury up the front in 1st Class. Well, we don't, and it is only the media that calls us 'oil executives'. We used to be a bit more pampered but nowadays it's down the back in the cheapest seat, somewhere near the rear toilets. We call it Cattle Class.

On a long haul flight such as the one from Cape Town to Johannesburg, Johannesburg to Perth and then Perth to Melbourne, it is a pain in the backside – literally. I was exhausted when I was picked up from the airport. I was tired and as usual after a long flight the first thing I wanted was a good shower and clean up. I was amazed when the guy who picked me up at the airport told me that a meeting had been arranged that very same morning. In fact I had only about one hour to dive into my hotel, quick shower and clean up, change of clothes and then sit in this long meeting feeling like a zombie and trying very hard to give an impression that I knew what I was talking about. Ha!

The next day was not too bad and we did manage to put a pretty good tender together over the next four or five days. Then I got my break – there was a discussion that since I was going to be hand-carrying this offer back into Mozambique and it was a couple of boxes of pretty hefty documents that maybe I should fly back 1$^{st}$ Class so I could keep the documents with me and not take the risk of them going missing in checked baggage.

'Good idea', I quickly added. You arrange it and pay for it and I will fly it.

Which they did.

So then it was the long trek back to J'Burg, but this time in luxury, and then onto Maputo.

That was interesting. It was the first time I had visited Mozambique although Joanne used to fly in there quite a bit when it was still Lourenco Marques. They have the best sea food in Southern Africa by the way.

But, dear me, it was a run down place. The civil war had just finished, or maybe it was just half time. The city itself was a run down mess. Sewage and rubbish in the streets and beggars everywhere. It was a sad sight. It was also not exactly stable yet and the only safe place to stay was in the Paloma Palace – Hey, I could get used to this jet set life. 1$^{st}$ Class flights everywhere and nothing less than 5 star hotels. Don't get too used to this Renwick as we are just about to have another change and it is certainly not 5 star.

I had hired a car in Maputo so I did take the opportunity to try and explore the place a bit but quite frankly the roads were in such a state and there was still a pervading sense of lawlessness that I did not stay too long and headed home. I think that was in early 1995 and I gather that it has changed considerably since then. In fact my step son, Sean, went there on holiday recently but since he is a bit wild anyway, that is no indication of how good it is now.

So after doing my thing in Maputo, I headed home.

Southern Africa was working pretty well and whenever you feel that things are ticking over quite nicely, look out as it is time for a change.

'Trevor, we want you to go back to Pointe Noire, Congo, to manage our operations there'.

Hey Ho – off we go.

# Congo – Again

By this time Congo was quite a big operation so it was not going to be the lean and mean experience I had when I had kicked the place off in '86.

Jo and I got organised and packed up our house in Paarl. Sean, Jo's son, was only about 19 at this stage and he was to complete a diploma in business management so he was going to have to stay and look after himself somehow. Jo arranged for him to stay at the Cape Town YMCA and he already had a little car (the obligatory first car, a Volkswagen Beetle) so we really did not have much choice. Jo had been through a lot of hardship with one thing and another and leaving Sean in Cape Town while we headed for Congo was going to be quite a wrench for her. But she didn't complain and arranged things in her usual capable efficient manner.

I was to go up to Pointe Noire first as there is always a lot to do at the very beginning and living in a hotel, and being stuck there all day – especially a hotel in Congo is a terrible experience.

So I would go up and get settled into my work and when our shipment was ready Jo would fly up to join me.

I was taking over the management from a chap who had somewhat different management style to me. Also, I suspect a different lifestyle.

When Jo joined me in Pointe Noire and after only a short few days in the hotel we went to check out the 'The Manager's House' – which sounds grand but in fact is just a small prefabricated bungalow in a dusty street. What was amazing when we got there, and we still laugh about it a lot, is that all the 'Staff' were there to greet us.

Have you ever seen one of those old British movies where

all the staff of the big country mansion are lined up outside to meet their new Lord or Lady or whatever?

It was like that – seriously. There was a 'House Manager' a day guard, a night guard, a cook, a cleaning lady, a gardener, a driver. This is ridiculous. It was a four bedroom pre-fabricated bungalow, for crying out loud. I bet the last manager's wife also had a little bell that was never far away, in case the Memsahib is in need of refreshment. Ha ha.

We kept a straight face and went through the introductions and pleasantries.

That evening we were still laughing about it. What in Heaven's name are we going to do with all these people. 'Maybe they can read to you if you feel tired.'

It took us about two months to farm these people out to other families and to any new families arriving so that they would not lose their chance to work.

Jo had never been to Congo before and it was nearly ten years since I had been there, so there was quite a bit of exploring to do and revisiting some old places. Before Jo arrived I had done a scouting trip up the coast to check the road and remind myself where some of the nicer places were. Quite a way along the coast there was this savannah type of land with rolling low hills and what looked like giant mushrooms – huge things. They were termite mounds or ant hills of course. So one of the first things we did when Jo got there was to take a drive around the countryside. It was incredibly important to me that Jo was happy there and I wanted her to like it. First impressions are important as they set the tone for any lengthy stay which is what I anticipated. I drove her up the same road to see these huge 'mushrooms' and we got out to have a look at them. Somewhere in the conversation it came out that they might be petrified. I replied that 'I was not afraid of mushrooms'. Lots of laughs and it is still one of Joanne's dinner party stories.

Our life in Congo was a busy round of work, fun parties and friends. We also ended up as the unofficial South Africa Embassy which is another amusing story. On our way back from a short local leave in South Africa a few months later, we had noticed a bunch of very Afrikaans looking farmer types boarding the same flight in J'Burg. You can spot them a mile off, huge stocky farmers in their kaki shorts. We also had heard that a group of South African farmers had moved into Congo and were going to try their hand at farming up there. Apparently this was some kind of effort by the Congolese government to try to resurrect the very neglected agriculture in Congo by offering free land to anyone that wanted to set up farms. I think this appealed to the farmers from South Africa. Another challenge and another trek. As we got off the plane in Brazzaville this same group of farmers with their wives and children was right behind us. Joanne and I were met by our agent in Brazzaville, Madame LeRoy (famous for her Gorillas) and she was already busy with the immigration department, processing our passports and papers. So we were just standing there waiting and you could see that this group of Afrikaans farmers were feeling a bit lost and did not know what to do next. So Jo went up to them and in her native Afrikaans asked them what they were doing there. You could see the look of relief flood over their faces. Here in the middle of nowhere was someone who spoke Afrikaans. They were so happy to see and speak to someone that it was quite an effort to get away. We gave them our contact numbers in Pointe Noire and told them that if ever they were down in Pointe Noire to look us up. Well, that opened the door didn't it. There were times when we had five or six of them living with us. Actually you can't blame them. The land they were trying to farm was about six hundred kilometres from the coast, in the middle of nowhere. There were no stores, no shops, no medical facilities. They were really on their own and I think that is what they wanted. They wanted to be self sufficient, like in the old trekking days. But they still had to buy some food stuffs and tools and some basic implements and that is when they descended on us in Point Noire.

It was good fun though and they appreciated it. In fact they invited me to visit them some time later when Jo was taking a short break in Paarl.

I was impressed with what they had achieved. They had been there about one year when I went to visit them. I flew up in an awful, old Russian aircraft, you know the type – you can see the rivets rattling in the wings, and landed on a dirt strip close to their local village. They were proud to show me the results of their first crop. They drove me around their fields and sure enough they had a good crop of maize and also sunflowers.

It all looked very good and there was certainly nothing wrong with the shear volume of their crops. The hassle was – where were they going to sell it, and to whom?

It seemed to me that this part of the equation had been missed out. There were no roads to speak of. There was a very old and dilapidated railway but that was miles away to the west. How on earth were they going to get this crop to market? Which market? Where?

One of the hassles of Africa. You can grow just about anything in West Africa but there is no infrastructure so you cannot do anything with what you grow. There is no point in going beyond subsistence farming.

I used to go down to Luanda in Angola quite a bit and you would see lots of UN aircraft unloading bags of flour and maize as part of their food aid programme and here, just across the river was a good crop that could not be delivered anywhere. What a shame. What a waste.

I did suggest that these farmers contact the UN and find out if there was a way they could supply their crops as part of the programme but I don't think anything happened about it.

Jo was also having 'Crop' problems. She loves gardening and trying to do something with our garden in Pointe Noire was a challenge. Just about anything would grow there. In fact you could put and old twig or stick in the ground and the next minute – up she came. Amazing. Part of the problem down on the coast though was the humidity. Every building and every wall had this black fungi type of growth on it. It looked like a black stain and there was no way of getting rid of it. The plants would get mouldy and it was a constant struggle to keep some plants healthy and to discourage others. But I think Jo enjoyed the challenge and in the end I would say that we had one of the nicest gardens there.

On with the tale.

Part of my job was to look after some operations we had going on in Zaire and also to get Soyo in Angola up and running again. So I used to fly around quite a bit and whenever possible I would take Jo with me. Most of my trips into Zaire were just day trips down the coast in a light aircraft so I would usually go on my own and I would usually be home for dinner. There was not much to see down there anyway.

You get to like West Africa if you don't mind the odd bit of hardship and the hassles that go with countries like these. The big advantage is that anything is possible if you know the right people or have made the appropriate 'consideration' to an official. It is actually quite refreshing to live in a country where rules and regulations are minimal.

One time Jo and I had been down to Luanda for a couple of days and on the way back up the coast the pilot turned round,

'Hey – are you guys thirsty?'

'Yes'

'Okay let's stop off in Muanda (that's in Zaire by the way) for a coke'

Okay – no problem. And it wasn't. Land, stretch the legs. Have a coke and take off again.

Wonderful.

Another time Jo and I were coming back from Luanda again. As we landed in Cabinda to let a couple of people off the plane, another small aircraft landed and stopped next to us. There was one of the Halliburton lads on board and he rushed across to our plane,

'Is Trevor on board?'

'Trevor we need you to come with us for a meeting in Zaire'

Okay – no problem. Step off one aircraft.

'Bye darling. See you back home for dinner.'

Hop on the other aircraft and off we went.

You see what I mean. Anything is possible there. Can you imagine trying to do that around Europe?

There is a tiny port in northern Angola called Soyo. Halliburton used to have a base there but it had been overrun in the civil war that raged on there for many years. I went down there to see what was left and see what would need to be done to get it back up and running again. It was a real mess. The military lads form UK and Australia and all over were still trying to clear the land mines and there was unexploded ordinance all over the place. There were some areas that had been cleared and so I was free to move around a bit. The areas still to be cleared were marked off with tape so it was fairly safe. The old Halliburton Base was stripped. Anything that could have been stolen had gone. Funnily enough the guerrillas had punched holes in the oil sumps of most of the trucks and

194

engines to use the oil for their own vehicles no doubt. I would have thought that they would just steal the whole truck. Maybe they could not get them started. There was one good side to the way they had stripped that base. They had taken every grain of cement and other dry powder material out of the silos we had there. They were absolutely spotless inside. I think you can imagine what would have happened to a tall silo full of cement left for five or six years in that humid climate. It would have been solid. So, all in all, not too bad.

What I needed now were a couple of willing helpers to start clearing the place up. I could not use any of the locals as there were still some civil war hassles and the area outside the base was still a bit unstable.

My step son, Sean, was still down in Cape Town. He had just finished his course and we think that he was getting close to going off the rails, as a lot of kids at that age can do. I suggested to Jo that Sean might be able to work in Soyo. What did she think? We both agreed that it was an opportunity for him and probably exactly what he needed.

I called him up that night and offered him the job.

'If we don't like you, we will fire you and if you don't like us you can walk away'. Do you remember that one?

Done deal – only condition is that I want you on an aircraft heading for Brazzaville tomorrow night. We will arrange the tickets and the visa on arrival. Just get yourself here.

Sure enough, next evening Sean was with us. Jo was very pleased and very proud and she still is. Sean has worked for Halliburton for over nine years now and I hear nothing but glowing reports. We are both proud of him.

I am sure that all this sounds very exciting and adventurous but there is a downside to this easy going, lack of controls and rules, type of existence. When you really need something doing quickly and efficiently – it does not happen.

The classic instance I am thinking of was when one of the lads in Pointe Noire became seriously ill with cerebral malaria. Poor Eliot had felt not too good the evening before but by morning he was in a very sad way. I did not know anything about this until I was told that Eliot was in the medical clinic. I got there at about 9.00 in the morning and by this time the poor lad was in a coma. That's how fast that damn disease strikes.

There was no option that I could see. If we didn't get him out of there to some good medical care, he was going to die. Full stop.

I rushed back to the office to get on our satellite phone and 'pressed the button' to get an air ambulance up from South Africa as that was the closest place for intensive care or whatever treatment Eliot might need.

There are quite a few hurdles to cross getting one of these air ambulances mobilised and on its way. Firstly, the doctors at each end have to talk to each other to make sure that the patient is seriously ill enough to warrant an air evacuation and on the other hand he must be in good enough condition to be able to be flown out. Fine balance sometimes.

Next, the air ambulance has to get clearance to fly up to Pointe Noire. That means getting clearance from South Africa, Namibia, Angola and then Congo. This all takes time and time is something I did not think we had a lot of.

On top of all this, the flying time from J'Burg to Pointe Noire was a good four hours and then there are the refuelling stops on top of that.

The last scheduled flight out of Pointe Noire used to be at about six o'clock in the evening and as soon as this flight has lifted its Dunlops off the tarmac the airport closes.

Immigration goes home, Customs go home, the Control Tower goes home – one empty airport.

I got news that the plane would be getting in at about 19.30 that evening so I had to go around every department at the airport to ask them to stay over. That needed a pocket full of money I can tell you.

So there we were, waiting at the airport that evening and sure enough at about 19.30 in comes this Lear Jet air ambulance. So far, so good. The medics on board then speak to the clinic by radio and give the okay for the patient to be brought to the airport by ambulance to board the plane. So far, so good. Customs have helped us out and we have got Eliot's passport already stamped and cleared. So far, so good. Nothing can go wrong – click – can go wrong – click – can go wrong – click.

Then the pilot asks 'where are the refuelling crew'? Their tanker is there and we had arranged for them to stay during this medivac but the crew are nowhere to be found.

Oh – no – bloody hell! We have a guy near to death and do you know what those idiots had done? They had gone off to a bar in town. Panic – which bar? – where? – for Christ's sake take my car and go and get them. What a palaver. Eventually, we got everything squared away and the ambulance arrived to load Eliot on board. Sophie, his girlfriend, was there and she asked me if she could go on the plane with Eliot. Of course – just rush over to immigration and get your passport stamped, get on board and we will look after the rest.

Which we did – As the Lear streaked down the runway and climbed steeply into the night skies I breathed a sigh of relief, sat down on a baggage trailer and lit up a cigarette. I had given up smoking a year before.

Eliot got to J'Burg and survived. He married Sophie and they now have two healthy kids. Nice end to that one.

Sadly, we were to go through a very similar evacuation only about six months later. This one did not have such a happy outcome. A good friend of ours, George, collapsed and had to be medivac'd out to J'Burg. He was still conscious as they loaded him onto the plane and he kept saying he would be fine.

He demanded that someone give him a cigarette and a beer and he would be okay. Unfortunately, that was not the case. He had suffered a cerebral haemorrhage and was not to recover. The company George worked for came to us and asked if Joanne could fly down to J'Burg to try to help with George's wife and family, which of course she did willingly. Sadly, she had to deal with a lot of emotional grief. He died in hospital just after his family got there from the UK. He was only 42.

Mother could not resist 'another country to explore' of course and came down for a holiday. I wonder how she dealt with the cocktail parties when she got home.

'Hello Betty. Where have you been?'

'I have been down to the Congo on holiday'

'Oh how nice. Do you know that Mrs. Smith's cat got run over again?'

We had a right old time while Mum was there as she was treated like royalty by all our friends. We also made it an excuse to have lots of functions for customers so she was wine'd and dine'd and generally spoilt. We even arranged a private train trip up into the central jungles. When I say 'private train' I think that I should qualify that. This was not a Pullman behind 'The Flying Scotsman'. The truth is that our 'train' was more like a bus on rails. Whatever. It could carry about twenty of us and we all piled on board early in the morning for our trip up country. Some of the more resilient guests came with pre-mixed gin and tonic in large water bottles. It was the usual Congo hot and humid day and by the time we got way up country half the passengers were very merry. There was no toilet on the train, well there was, but it was not working, so whenever we needed to we would ask the driver to stop and then climb down and head off into the jungle.

We had a lovely lunch in a village way up in the central

highlands with more wine and booze. It was going to be a very long day.

The only thing that spoilt this little expedition was that some of the locals were trying to sell us a baby gorilla and that was a bit heart wrenching. To buy it off them would just encourage the market and the poor chap's chances of survival were minimal unless someone took care of it. As soon as we got back to Point Noire I called Madame LeRoy at her gorilla sanctuary in Brazzaville to let her know. She did actually manage to rescue the poor animal and get it down to Pointe Noire but sadly it died shortly afterwards.

There is also one of Jane Goodall's chimpanzee sanctuary's close to Pointe Noire and we took Mum up to see that and to visit the very special Belgian lady that lives up there in the middle of nowhere looking after them. Nice experience and interesting.

We made many friends in Pointe Noire and I am happy to say that we stay in touch with most of them. It was an interesting and enjoyable assignment. Joanne and some of her friends even organised an art exhibition to show off their work. We rented a room at the wonderful Sea Club restaurant and hung the paintings and arranged for classical music to be playing quietly in the background. It was a great success and we had to extend the exhibition for three days as so many people wanted to see it. Who said that the Congo was a cultural vacuum.

On the work side the Congo was doing fine so it was about time to move on again. We had been living there for three years and as Jo and I are gipsies at heart we were starting to get itchy feet. Jo had been quite sick with malaria and then a parasitic bug that would not go away and we had a whole life to catch up on. Decision time – All vote for getting out of here – Yeahhh.

Where to next? Well these things do not always happen

overnight. You have to send out the feelers. Find out where your friends and mentors are. Get out the world map and list your priorities.

Opening in Venezuela eh? Ummh – Interesting. Maracaibo eh?. Ummh – Never been there before.

So that's what we did. I had accepted a position as manager of what we call 'Zonal Isolation' for Northern Venezuela. Sounds grand doesn't it? If I translate that for you it comes out that I will manage the cementing services part of the Halliburton work for the area around Lake Maracaibo and some outlying bases we had to the west and south of there. There that's clearer isn't it. To be truthful, 'Cementing' is quite high tech as you have to pump some pretty fancy cement slurries into the wells as they are drilled to isolate the different formations as you drill through them and to support the steel casings in the wells. Our high tech logging or reservoir mapping lads call cementers 'Sack Rippers' but that is not really fair. Now, that's enough of the tech stuff Trevor. Get on with the story.

# VENEZUELA

So it was pack up time again. There was no big problem to pack up our house in the Congo and have all our furniture and belongings shipped to Venezuela. The hassle was our dog 'Lady'. We had flown her up from South Africa to Congo without too much of a problem but now she would have to go a long, round about route and have to stay in kennels somewhere until we got a house arranged and got our shipment. We arranged to fly her up to Paris and as it was winter up there we organised for her to stay in heated kennels. What a spoilt animal. It ended up costing us a fortune, but what do you do?

We took a break in South Africa to give a little more time for the shipment to get to Venezuela. Then it was head off and go time. We flew up to Miami and then down on a really worn out, dirty, rattly old Boeing 727 to Maracaibo. We were about eight hours late when we took off from Miami so it was the middle of the night by the time we landed in Maracaibo. There was a driver there to collect us and take us down to Las Morochas which was about 100 kilometres down the west side of the lake along the Via Communal, or Via Criminal, as we learnt to call it later. The driver picked up our bags and led us to his vehicle. I do not know what he used this vehicle for normally as it was not a taxi. It was a fluffy panel van. You know, one of those big Ford or Chevy touring things. The difference was that this one was kitted out. It had three inch thick pink pile carpet throughout. A couple of fluffy pink armchairs. It was amazing. I think it must double as a travelling bordello.

Hey – beggars can't be choosers so we climbed in and set off for Las Morochas.

We were booked into the only hotel in Las Morochas but by the time we got there it was about one in the morning. It was dead. We were tired, hungry and thirsty but room service was a bit above this hotel. We struggled to get someone to understand that even a bottle of water would do. What a miserable first night in Venezuela.

Poor Jo ended up spending about a month in that hotel and it was no fun. The one bright spot was that Sean was up in the US doing some training so he came to join us and all three of us ended up stuck in that hotel.

Things have way or working out and sure enough the time came for our shipment to be delivered. So it was house preparation time and also buy the electrical items we needed.

All our electrical stuff from South Africa and Congo was 220 volts but Venezuela is 110 volts so that was bit of fun. We had to buy everything, literally, brand new. The poor store manager did not speak a word of English, we did not speak Spanish, so we had a right old time making him understand we needed a whole household of electrical goods. It made his day, maybe even his month!

We had another wonderful, funny experience with languages a short time after we had moved in.

We went to the butcher to buy some lamb. Butchers shops in Venezuela are more like coffee shops. You sit at stools at a bar and you have a cup of coffee or a brandy or whatever, as you chat to the butcher and tell him what you want. He then goes into the cool rooms and takes out whatever it is you want and then cuts the joint or piece you want right there on the counter top in front of you.

Jo and I knew where this particular butcher shop was but it wasn't until we got there that we realised we did not know the word for 'lamb'. We had learnt very early on how to say:

'How do you say xxxxx' etc,. 'Como se dice xxxxxx' etc., Usually you can point to something and 'como se dice' will get the required Spanish translation. But in this butchers shop there was nothing to point at and not knowing the correct word I blurted out,

'Como se dice Merrrrr' – As in the sound of a lamb – in case that was not too clear.

The whole place erupted into laughter. Everyone was enjoying the sight of this Englishman trying to speak Spanish. It was all very good hearted and after more cups of coffee and one sided conversations with the butcher and his customers we left with our 'leg of lamb' . To tell you the truth we were never quite sure if we left with lamb or goat.

A serious effort was made by both of us to learn Spanish. We got in contact with a teacher who was recommended to us, Dolly. We went there three evenings a week and then went home like good little kids and did our homework together. Jo became very good at it and can still sprout forth in Spanish if she wants. Impressive.

And so was Dolly. Impressive is the word I would use. She definitely left an impression.

She would wear the shortest little mini skirts and she could as she had good legs and she used to wear the lowest cut, tight, blouses for the same sort of reason. She was not a very tall girl so she would stretch to write on her blackboard. She would also lean over her desk intently to read from her text book. Oh dear me. My Spanish would become French and the occasional Swedish or even Arabic would get in there. She was deliberately sabotaging my efforts to learn Spanish. She was fun though and she knew exactly what she was doing and became a very regular and popular guest at our parties.

Las Morochas was a noisy, busy little town and it had some really nice restaurants. Surprisingly there were also a bunch of our friends who had moved over from Congo who were working in the oil industry around that area. So the social life was quite hectic and fun. Work was pretty easy after the hassles of West Africa and my responsibilities were not as great, so life was ticking over quite nicely.

While we were there we had a visit from some dear friends from South Africa, Francois and Ilona. The poor devils were locked up in Miami as they did not have a visa to transit the US. That seemed really dumb to me. You do not even leave the airport but the US will not allow you to transit through to catch another aircraft without a visa. They got in alright, but had a hell of a job getting out of Venezuela at the end of their stay as no airline would take them without a US visa. What a mess. Hey – we managed it eventually with the help of South African Airlines.

We took this opportunity of their visit to do a bit of exploring and had a wonderful time. We flew out to the island of Aruba which is just off the coast and Francois and I made idiots of ourselves trying to parasail behind a power boat in a twenty knot wind. While Francois was up there two hundred feet above the boat in the howling wind Ilona got hold of a knife and threatened to cut the rope. All good fun and quite an experience for Francois as he had not travelled much. We went diving and sailing and generally gave them a bit of a spoily. I have no idea why Aruba is such a popular destination with Americans as there is nothing there and it is one of the most unattractive Caribbean islands I have ever been on. I think it has something to do with the 24 hour casinos there. Shame.

Next destination was way up in the Andes Mountains and that was also great. What an experience.

Joanne and I also had the ultimate spoily for ourselves. Jerry and Rebecca from Congo were in Venezuela as Jerry was the new general manager for quite a big oil company out there.

We got on well together so we decided to take a trip together to see Angel falls. The highest waterfall in the world. Wow – There were no roads in or out of the south eastern part of Venezuela so we went in by air and spent one night at a rather primitive hotel / camp by a huge waterfall. The next morning we piled into long canoes with outboard engines and set off up river. We were part of a group and there were three of these canoes with about eight to ten people in each one. The scenery was spectacular with high flat topped mountains all around and the river weaving and snaking its way through them and around them. It was a long five hour run to get to the base of Angel Falls and then it was an hour slog up through the rain forest to get to a precarious ledge where you got the best view.

We could not see the top of the falls as the mountain rose straight up into the clouds. It was quite spooky really as this huge water fall was coming down out of the clouds. We just sat and stared at this incredible sight. Not a word was spoken. It was spell binding.

Beautiful. Awesome.

You might be able to gather from these stories of our time in Las Morochas that I was taking life easy. In a way that is true as this was a doddle compared to managing somewhere like Congo or Algeria. I think that both Jo and I agree that we had more fun in Congo but we were both 'African' so we probably felt more at home there. Anyway, our time in Las Morochas was going to be limited. I must have impressed someone somewhere as I got a phone call asking me if I would accept a position on the Latin America North Leadership team. In hindsight I should have said no.

I must be careful what I say here as Halliburton will sue the living daylights out of me if I am not careful. Some bright spark high up in Halliburton had an idea to change the management structure of our regional centres, such as Middle East, Far

East, Africa, Europe etc. to a flat management team structure. Amazingly this was modelled on a self management system that British coal miners devised at the coal face as they had no communications with the outside world. I don't know which management guru thought this one up but I personally would strangle him if I ever came face to face. There are so many of these management gurus floating around that there is always a risk that your company might suddenly buy into some hair brained scheme that costs the company an absolute fortune and is destined to failure before it even starts. That was what I got involved in.

I was cunningly invited to join the team looking after our business in Venezuela, Colombia and Ecuador. I would look after the famous 'Zonal Isolation' in these countries and other members of this team would each have their own respective areas of expertise to manage. There would be about six of us on this flat management team and there would be no team leader or general manager. Decisions would be made on a team basis.

Oh dear me. I am afraid that if I had fully understood what I was about to get involved with I would have backed out of it there and then. My meteoric rise through the ranks of Halliburton was just about to come to an abrupt end.

As you might be able to gather from the tale so far, I tend to do my own thing and I am afraid my temperament and personality was not going to rest happily in this new high-powered management team. My first conflict with this rather strange set up was when we were told to gather at a rather plush five star hotel in Caracas where we would stay for about four days to go through regional planning and team building. By this time Joanne and I had moved up from Las Morochas and we had rented a nice apartment in the centre of Caracas.

The hotel where these meetings were to take place was only a twenty minute drive from our apartment. So, when the powers that be said that I was booked to stay in this hotel I politely told them that this would not be necessary. It was pointed out to me that I was missing the point. The whole idea of staying at the hotel was for this new management team to spend as much time together as possible and to get to know each other better. I was not impressed.

'If you think that I am going to stay in this hotel buying people beers and hugging them you have another thing coming. I am married to my wife, not to Halliburton.'

I did not exactly start off on the right foot did I ?

Then there were the endless meetings in Houston. I am not very good at that either.

I find it quite amusing to sit at these meetings and listen. I am afraid that there are not too many independent souls left out there. I am not good at company jargon or buzz words or phrases and I would sometimes listen to the most mindless presentations as someone with ambition (you remember my comments from my days at Durham) would tailor his presentation and comments to what he thought the company leadership wanted to hear.

Sad. And beware anyone who dares to question. Very sad.

I only stayed in that job for about six months but that was enough time for Jo and I to head off to Colombia and Ecuador. I was attending meetings in Bogotá and the Halliburton team there were kind enough to arrange some sight seeing for Jo. We were staying at the lovely Moneypenny Hotel in town which was super and every evening we were invited out to some of the fabulous restaurants in town. Very nice. We liked Bogotá.

Then we flew down to Ecuador for more meetings in Quito. We flew in at night through some pretty severe weather and we could feel the plane banking quite steeply as it made its approach into Quito. The pilot slammed the plane down on the tarmac and he had every brake and reverse thrust on maximum as he brought the plane to a stop. Blimey – that was a bit rough we thought. Not to worry, off we go to the Hilton hotel in town and put our heads down. It had been a long day.

The next morning the skies had cleared and as we looked out of the hotel window we realised why the pilot had been a bit heavy on the controls. The airport at Quito is a tiny short strip in the middle of town and all around are the sharp peaks of the Andes as well as the nearby volcanoes. Oh blimey – thank God we did not know that as we had come in to land as there was very little room for an aircraft to manoeuvre. Quito airport actually has quite a bad reputation for aircraft crashing or going off the end of the runway. Happily we were blissfully unaware of that at the time.

Again it was a nice mixture of meetings for me and sight seeing for Jo. We explored Quito as much as we could and after a couple of days of meetings we had set aside a day or two to have a driver take us round some of the countryside. Fantastic. We both treasure those memories and Ecuador is one of our favourite places. Wonderful people, stunning scenery and just one nice place.

But the wheels were turning. While we were in Quito I got a call from Houston to go there as soon as possible. I think I had a premonition that this was not going to be another promotion. I had reached my level of incompetence and the bosses were not impressed with my way of doing things. Whooops. You see, my little pea brain had failed to understand what was expected of me. In Africa I was expected to run the show, make decisions and generally stand on my own two feet. In this new lofty position I was expected to conform and to act as the mouthpiece of our illustrious leaders. It was more important in this position to spread the good word of the latest thinking in Mission Statements and Company Visions. I was there to conform and I did not realise it. Shame on you Renwick lad. I really was out of my depth.

The bosses also have a very subtle way of getting their message across. Normally, when I went to Houston I would be booked into one of the rather nice 5 star hotels but when I got there this time I was told that I was booked in at a hotel that I had never heard of and neither had the taxi driver. We went round and round and eventually found it tucked away in a not very attractive part of town. It was one of those cheapy, small, self service types of hotel that you would imagine travelling salesmen stay at. I don't know how many stars it had but it would have struggled to get two in Europe. This is not what I am used to! What happened to the five star treatment?

I found out next morning when I went into the office to see the big boss. The guy was pleasant enough but the message was clear. Go pack your bags. Find a job if you can, but you are off this team.

I think that I was secretly quite glad this was over. I had not really enjoyed what I was doing and I am afraid that the higher I got to the top of the pile the less respect I had for our leaders. Get me out of here!

The problem now was that I was not in a good position to just step aside and find a new job. I was not the flavour of the month in Houston and there did not seem to be a lot of effort being made to slot me back into my lower level of competency. I could not afford to retire and it was essential that I keep an income stream going. Time to touch base with all my old buddies and mentors. Help!

There was a subconscious panic going on I suppose. Here I was aged some fifty two years old with nowhere to go. At that age you are not exactly on the top of the recruitment list if you try to change jobs. You are also on the downhill side of the career path. As it was I ended up with quite a few offers from different regions within the Halliburton world and I was able to weigh up the pro's and con's of a few good offers. A couple of them were quite complimentary but I could see myself back into the same position that I had just got out of. One was to be manager in UK for one of the operational departments but that would have meant going to live in the UK and the dreadful reality of having to pay taxes. Ahhhh!

I think that when you are in one of these subconscious panic modes you tend to retreat to a world you know and understand. For me that was Africa and by pulling a few strings I was offered a position back in Algeria in the Business Development department which sounds great but is just basically sales and marketing. Hey, I can do that – lead me on.

It was also in an area that had some security problems and as such there were no live in positions and everyone commutes in and out on a four weeks on and four weeks off basis.

Jo and I decided that we can live with that and might actually have more quality time together. Six months off per year and get paid for it. Yes – that should be okay.

Everyone who hears that we work one month on and one month off seems to think that this must be great. Only working six months a year – Wow – How do I get a job like that?

I suggest that you have a think about that for a while. You work for four weeks with no weekends off, seven days per week and usually long hours as there is nothing much else to do. No public holidays. Working Christmas and New Year if you end up on the wrong schedule and for me the worse bit is curling up in bed on my own with my wife six thousand miles away, also curling up to sleep on her own – we hope.

I really believe that if you tally up the hours worked on one of these rotational schedule jobs you will find they are a lot higher than a normal job, living at home.

That's really why Jo and I prefer the live-in jobs. The other great advantage of Live-In jobs is that you get to know the country you are in very well. You are not just a one month tourist. I like that. It is all clear now isn't it? I miss my wife.

# ALGERIA – AGAIN

So Algeria it was. I went off to London for about three weeks of meetings and planning which was very boring. London is not my favourite place on earth. Then off I went again to Algeria for the third time. 'Hello lads – me again'.

The Sahara was not the Sahara I knew from the old days when we were free to travel around. In those days we would even take the embassy people down on camping trips into the middle of the huge sand dunes areas and spend hours searching for arrow heads or just having fun driving through the dunes in our 4x4's. This new Algeria was very restricted. There had been quite a few terrorists incidents and quite a few expats had been killed so security was now tight. Whenever we travel out of the main base we have to have a military escort and going on camping trips is definitely not on. Shame, as it is a beautiful country.

But we are well looked after in our fancy big camp, so being locked up is not too bad. We all have our little single rooms with shower and toilet and a satellite TV to watch, so life could be worse. Our rooms are cleaned by ladies from the local town of Hassi Messaoud and our laundry is done on the base. This is building up into another 'funny' isn't it?

At work I usually wear a pair of lace up brown work boots and I have a habit, handed down from my father, of polishing my boots regularly. I keep a tin of dark tan shoe polish in my room and every so often I will wash the dust off my boots and give them a polish. One day I could not find the little brush that I use for this so I was looking around for a rag or cloth. There was an old pair of white underpants that the laundry had destroyed. The elastic had gone and they were destined for the bin. Ahha, that will do the trick. So I sat there diligently putting this dark tan shoe polish onto my boots with this old pair of underpants. When I finished I thought that I will give them a bit of a rinse off and I can use them as my shoe polish rag in future. So I washed them under the tap and then hung them over the towel rail to dry. The next morning I forgot to put them away. I completely forgot about them and then I could not understand why my room had not been cleaned. It actually took a couple of days before it dawned on me why my room was being ignored. You can imagine the poor cleaning lady walking into my room and seeing these stained pair of underpants hanging there in the bathroom – ahhhaaa! Filthy infidels!

The actual work for me in Algeria was quite easy and apart from the odd lump of hard work with tenders and contracts it was not too demanding. So I just ticked over and did what I had to do. It was not quite as exciting as in the early days as there was a lot more control from the US than before. Also, with e-mail and the Internet you spend most of your time sitting in front of a computer. I think that this in itself causes some problems as our leaders in the USA do not need to travel so much and I feel that in some ways they and the teams in the US have lost touch with international operations and they sometimes forget how important it is to be aware of, and respect, different cultures and different societies. They try to impose American standards and American culture into a foreign environment and then do not understand why it does not work. We had one classic example with a new Halliburton Web Site that was first called myHalliburton.com. So far, so good. It was a good site for looking up technical information and equipment specifications and other work related subjects. I was the local supervisor of this web site and it was my job to introduce customers to the site and to show them how to use it.

Then just after the attack on the World Trade Centre in 2001 there was a lot of patriotic flag waving going on in the USA, and quite right. There was also a lot of right wing aggression and a focus on military subjects and CIA intelligence and all that hype that goes with any build up to war or aggression. It was at this stage that some bright spark in Texas, who had obviously never travelled and did not realise that half our international operations are in sensitive areas, decided to change the name of myHalliburton to 'Intelligence Central'. That was only the start of the problems. They then said that all local focal points for this web site would now be called 'Agents'. This is getting silly, and it got sillier. They then informed us that they would be sending out black Tee shirts for each 'Agent' and what size did we want to order. The last straw was that these Tee shirts were going to have the company logo on them and 'Intelligence Central – Agent' embroidered on them in white cotton. You have really got to be joking. Can you imagine walking through downtown Algiers or Kuwait or anywhere, with 'Intelligence Central – Agent' blazoned on your chest. Ridiculous, and I said so. I think that this idea was dropped pretty quickly. But it does go to show how out of touch some people are with the realities and risks of international life.

With the new travel and security restrictions in Algeria there was not much to do in the evenings so a buddy of mine, Peter, and I decided that we should make an area where we could play, or practice golf. Our first attempt was to just hit the balls off the sand. One giant bunker. But that didn't work. The sand is too fine and it was like trying to play the ball in a big bowl of flour. Dust everywhere.

Plan B. We got about ten drums of old sump oil from the mechanics and poured it onto some piled up sand to make a tee off area. That didn't work either. The oil sank in about one inch and that was all. That was really strange. We had put a lot of oil down and it just seemed to be absorbed by the sand and really only put an oily skin on the surface. The club heads and our boots were covered with oil and sand and just below the surface we were back to dust again.

Plan – C., The cementing dept had a few new trainees and they needed some practice mixing and pumping cement slurries so we set up a new area and put some boarding round it to hold the cement in place and – Bingo, we had our concrete Tee Off area. Next came a very old dilapidated cabin which was donated by one of the departments. Then one of our customers, Total, donated some driving mats with Astro Turf in them. I brought in some clubs to get going and there we had it. The start of what was to become a very famous facility in Algeria. The Sahara Golf & Country Club. A bit tongue in cheek as it is or was more than basic. It became really quite popular and so we started by having a membership fee which was 50 old golf balls. It was somewhere to go in the evenings and it was quite good practice for your golf as we had over two hundred metres of range to play with.

At this stage I would not say that we had tamed the Sahara but there was a small group of us that got an enormous amount of pleasure from this golf club. Each trip we would plan some new improvement or some new extension. We went through a step change at the club when we decided to put in a pond. Another of our customers, Anadarko, had donated a huge plastic pit liner so apart from the hole in the ground we had everything we needed for a water feature. There was a digger machine in the base one day so with a bit of bribery and corruption in the form of a Halliburton cap we had our hole dug out in next to no time. Next step was to unwrap the pit liner. It had been delivered in a very large box so this was not some little plastic sheet for a pond at the back of a house in Great Ayton. This was a monster black sheet used by drilling rigs to contain their used drilling muds. This thing was as big as two football pitches, and it was a windy day Ha Ha. There were six of us trying to spread this sheet out with the wind getting under it and lifting us off our feet as we hung on to this huge, billowing, black monster. The bloody thing was alive – and strong too. What

215

a circus! But we eventually got it folded double and cut to a reasonable size and place into the new hole in the ground. That was easy. Fill with water. See where the overflow goes, bit of adjustment. Done.

The making of this little pond became the catalyst for a non stop series of improvements which still continue today. Young Trevor (I am Old Trevor ) decided that we had enough pit liner left so the next year another much bigger pond was made. Quite nice actually as the small pond at the top overflows into the bigger one down a small series of steps which were another improvement.

Trees have been planted down each side of the driving range. Irrigation systems have been installed. Night floodlights have been hooked up. Our old cabin now has a large wooden deck in front of it which was salvaged from a large shipping palette. It is rather a swish place. We also have lovely green lawns going down to the edge of the ponds and recently we planted circles of grass out on the range to act as greens. Not exactly putting quality but they look good and have now survived two hot Sahara summers so as long as they get water they should be fine.

One of the funny stories associated with our Sahara Golf & Country Club is the story behind the goldfish we now have in the ponds. When we built the first pond we decided that it would be nice to have some fish in it. We did some research and found out that goldfish could survive the very hot summers and the cold winters and so that's what we should go for. We needed to find a shop that could supply these fish as near as possible to Gatwick so that they would only have a short three hour flight to contend with. On the way back to South Africa at the end of that tour of duty I scouted out the route from Gatwick up to Victoria looking for a suitable suburb near to a train station that might have a pet shop. Sure enough there was a town called Balham that looked close so I made a note to stop off there on my way back into Algeria in four weeks time.

Four weeks later back I came, laden with fish food from my local shop in Paarl and some instruction and guidance of what type of fish to buy. I had brought a large two litre plastic bottle with a wide neck with me, so I was fully prepared. Taking the underground from Heathrow and then a commuter train from Victoria had me heading in the right direction – Balham.

I had never been to Balham before but I knew the name of the place from the famous Peter Sellers skit – Balham – Gateway to the South. Now I knew why Sellers had chosen Balham and now I knew why I would never be going back there. What a depressingly awful place. Half the shops are boarded up and there is a sense of despair and poverty about the place. It gives the impression of a town that has given up even trying. Sad.

It was also one of those cold windy days which added to the depression of the place.

I wandered down this cold, empty high street and found a baker's shop open with a very plump friendly looking lady behind the counter. I don't suppose Balham gets a lot of visitors and there I was carrying my brief case and my overnight bag with a pretty good South African summer sun tan asking this kind lady in the bakers shop where could I buy some goldfish. I am sure that she did a double take on this. Another crazy let loose in the streets of Balham. I tried explaining but I think I just made matters worse.

'Actually I am on my way to the Sahara Desert and I want to buy some goldfish for a pond we have there'.

See what I mean ?

As the day progressed there was a serious risk that I was going to be locked up and put into one of those white canvas jackets – with ropes!

Those nice young men in their clean white coats – they're coming to take me away, ha ha.

The lady in the baker's shop kept her distance and directed me to a pet shop in Tooting Broadway which was only one station away on the underground.

Off I went and sure enough I found the pet shop and explained what I wanted and why. Again the funny looks but I think the guy serving me eventually realised that I was harmless and we discussed the number of fish to buy, the size, the length of the flight and how long would it be before I could put them in the pond. How to put them in the pond so any temperature change did not shock them. This was some pretty serious forward planning going on here. Goldfish must not be taken lightly you know.

We decide that ten fish might be pushing it a bit so we settled on five. The shop owner explained that the bottle should be only 2/3 full to allow some oxygen into the water and he added a couple of tablets of something-or-other that would keep the fish calm, and plop – in they went, all five, little baby goldfish. I stuffed the bottle into my carry-on flight bag and set off for Gatwick feeling very pleased with myself.

Obviously, I had to take the bottle and the fish in my carry-on baggage as I don't think they would survive in the baggage hold and being bashed around by the baggage handlers. I calmly went through the security checks and placed the bag with the poor fish hidden inside onto the X-Ray screening machine. I could see that the guy on the security screening machine had seen something of interest as he called his colleagues and they all bent over the monitor. I thought – this is it – but no, they looked and looked and then just let me go. I wonder what they saw – does the monitor show moving objects swimming around in a bottle?

Okay – so far so good. The next step was to make sure that these poor fish had as much oxygen as possible. So I sat down in the departures area, opened my bag and took the top off the bottle and started blowing gently into the bottle to give the poor little creatures some fresh air. Gatwick is a busy airport and I suppose that if you see someone sitting with his bag on the table and he is blowing into this bag it might raise a few eyebrows.

But there again Gatwick has quite a lot of rather strange people going through it so maybe this was just another normal day.

The Algerian customs did not even see the bottle, so as soon as I got to the base I took our little imports down to the pond and gradually introduced them to their new home.

As always these types of simple projects tend to mushroom and the next hurdle to tackle was how to encourage these fish to breed. Various suggestions were made such as throwing a Viagra tablet into the pond but eventually a visiting engineer who professed to knowing something about goldfish volunteered his advise. He noted that the pond now had a gravel bottom and rocks along the sides and he told us that goldfish did not like to breed in such harsh surroundings. He kindly informed us that what we should do is to place a string mop head in the pond, which would give the fish a softer spot in which to breed. This priceless piece of information was not taken too seriously. However, on my return to Paarl I was visiting the pet shop again to buy some more fish food and in discussions with the shop owner on the welfare of goldfish, the subject of breeding came up. Without hesitation the owner of the shop told me that goldfish did not like to breed in a rocky environment and that we should place a string mop head in the pond which would give them a soft spot in which to breed. I am not a man that has to be told twice, so it was straight down to the supermarket to choose the 'breeding mop', which now has place of honour in the pond in the Sahara. And it worked. When I went back on a later trip into Algeria I was confronted by members of the Sahara Golf & Country Club, congratulating me on being a

'Daddy'. There are now so many fish in these ponds that I have given up counting. We did add some more fish to give the gene pool a boost but apart from feeding them every evening they seem to thrive.

Our little Sahara Golf & Country Club has kept us busy and for several years all of us would bring items in that we needed. Fish food, irrigation fittings, grass seed, pumps, you name it we hand carried it in. It really is quite a picture now and many people comment on the quality of the grass and the size of the fish and the general soothing effect that this oasis in the middle of the Sahara has on everyone. The Algerian staff call it a 'Miracle' and I suppose in some ways it is. We even discovered that the Algerian Airports Authority had taken a picture of our club and they put this photograph on the inside cover of their official brochure with the caption, 'Who would believe you could find such a piece of paradise in Hassi Messaoud'. I am quite proud of that.

The locals and our guys who have been in Algeria for a long time understand what a 'Miracle' it is to have a golf club with ponds, grass and fish but it is sometimes lost on our less well travelled visitors.

We had a visit from a senior Vice President from Houston and when he saw this club he said, 'Oh a golf driving range – we have a lot of these in Houston'.

Shame – Kind'a missed the point. You have to feel sorry for them really.

# AND NOW?

We are now up to date. November 2005 and it has been fun. So there we have it. 59 years crammed into about 220 pages. That's a bit sad when you think about it. But you will have gathered by now that I have left a lot out. Not suitable for younger readers or sensitive souls and all that. I keep on remembering other funny or interesting incidents so I might have to write a sequel to fill in the tantalising gaps. Some of the other stories or tantalising gaps will never be told or put into print, so you will just have to use your imagination to fill them in. Maybe we can wait another ten years or so and come up with The Lighthouse Keeper II.

These last eleven years with Jo have been my reward for being patient and waiting those 47 years to find my soul mate. My only regret is the need to keep working and spending time away from home. But it does keep the money rolling in and my time off at home in Paarl does give me the opportunity to follow some of my hobbies such as restoring old cars, the odd bit of clay pigeon shooting. Hey, I even went horse riding for the first time in many a long year about six months ago, and it was not a short little walk around a paddock either. This was six hours in the saddle, up into the mountains behind Paarl. I couldn't cross my legs for three days after that effort.

So we are looking forward to the day I can retire but that is based on the Lottery so I might have to be patient. But Jo and I are healthy enough so I think we have quite a few more years to enjoy ourselves. We both like to travel and explore and I think that I will give aeroplanes a break for a few months and travel around in South Africa as there is a lot I still have not seen.

We also have that wonderful property up on the West Coast which we love. We still only have that thirty year old caravan parked behind the sand dunes but it suits us. We actually have plans for a small house up there and with a bit of luck we might be able to start building this year.

Right now we are in the process of moving house from Paarl to Hermanus. Guess what my mother said?

'Oh how nice a new place to explore'

Jo and I are both gypsies at heart and do you know what – when we were discussing our need to move on again and our love of privacy and nature there is one place that would suit us down to the ground.

## A Lighthouse

Not the End

Printed in the United States
by Baker & Taylor Publisher Services